THE HEART OF THE GOSPEL

The True Therapy For The Human Soul

By

Simmone Boothe

Published by New Generation Publishing in 2023

Copyright © Simmone Boothe 2023

First Edition

The author asserts the moral right under the Copyright, Designs and Patents Act 1988 to be identified as the author of this work.

All Rights reserved. No part of this publication may be reproduced, stored in a retrieval system or transmitted, in any form or by any means without the prior consent of the author, nor be otherwise circulated in any form of binding or cover other than that which it is published and without a similar condition being imposed on the subsequent purchaser.

ISBN   978-1-83563-140-9

www.newgeneration-publishing.com

New Generation Publishing

This book is dedicated to:

To you the reader, as you continue on your journey to seek the true meaning of life

Table of Contents

Prologue (or Monologue) 1

Introduction... 3

PART I: Laying the Foundation 5

    Chapter 1: Creation vs Evolution: A Matter of Faith..6

    Chapter 2: Faith: Essential Evidence in Science 10

    Chapter 3: Nature of Man: Part Spirit, Part Physical 14

PART 2: Nature 19

    Chapter 1: Beginnings.....................................20

    Chapter 2: Understanding the Male and the Female 25

    Chapter 3: Attachment: Why We Need It 30

    Chapter 4: Taking a Quick Look at our Physical Nature 35

    Chapter 5: We are Relational Beings 40

PART 3: Disconnected 45

    Chapter 1: The Emotional and Psychological Effects of Disconnection 46

    Chapter 2: What we have Inherited.................52

Chapter 3: What we have Inherited: Rebellion 57

Chapter 4: What we have Inherited: Narcissism 65

Chapter 5: What we have Inherited: Shame and Guilt 72

Chapter 6: What we have Inherited: Rejection and Fear 79

PART 4: The Gospel as the Cure 93

Chapter 1: Our Need for a Saviour God 94

Chapter 2: Why Evil and Suffering Exist 97

Chapter 3: Living Temples and Sacrifices ... 103

Chapter 4: The Human Body is a Temple 110

Chapter 5: Justification: Wiping the Slate Clean 115

Chapter 6: Sanctification: The Divine Image Restored 122

Chapter 7: The Power of Forgivness 130

Prologue (or Monologue)

Today, more than ever, with our modern-paced living and rapid changes, life has become more uncertain, negatively affecting our physical and mental health. Therapy is the growing trend people are turning to in order to cope. But did you know that at the heart of the gospel message lies the true therapy for the human soul?

The sincere aim of the gospel message is to highlight the natural state of the human heart and its need for reconciliation and connection with God first, then with others, and with oneself.

Over time, the heart of the gospel message has been obscured under the mire of self-righteousness, formality, conformity, double standards, and hypocrisy, causing people to turn away from wanting to hear the gospel or finding an alternative to what the world can offer.

Psychology and psychiatry attempt through secular means to address the symptoms of unmet emotional and psychological needs, but they are unable to fully address the root cause as they deny or discount the spiritual nature of man.

This book intends to address this gap. As a mental health practitioner and accredited therapist, I have had the privilege of supporting people with varying diagnoses of personality, anxiety, and mood disorders. No matter what the diagnostic label assigned, in each person is found the negative emotional and psychological states of fear, narcissism, rebellion, rejection, guilt, and shame.

Medication, meditation, and other self-help strategies can ease some of the symptoms caused by these negative emotional and psychological states, but they cannot address the root cause as to why they are in the human heart, and how they can be truly resolved.

No matter who you are or what you believe, I am sure that you will find something of benefit in these pages to help you as you journey through life. Please accept my invitation and come on in...

Simmone

Introduction

Every good therapy should start with laying a foundation, which usually consists of building a therapeutic relationship, understanding the nature of the presenting issues, and working in collaboration to provide solutions and strategies to alleviate symptoms.

I am hoping that as you continue to read on, a relationship will develop between you and me, even though we are not in direct communication. At the start of therapy sessions, there is usually an assessment process where problematic emotional or psychological symptoms such as anxiety or depression are identified along with their impact on daily life. Historical information is gathered to determine the onset and probable causes. Finally, goals or aims are discussed to provide a focus for change and containment for the therapeutic process, which can easily go off track, something that is unhelpful for both client and therapist.

As I author this book, I intend to replicate this method in how this book is planned or laid out. Each section hopefully will build on the previous one to give you a full picture or idea of how and why the Gospel Message is the true therapeutic approach needed for the human soul. I also hope this approach will highlight how true science and true faith (there are counterfeits of each, unfortunately) blend perfectly together and are not as antagonistic as they may initially appear.

There will be repetition in each of the chapters. This is intentional, to build understanding and knowledge which is necessary when presenting a new way of viewing things. Repetition also brings clarity and removes ignorance, a major factor in the maintenance of mental dis-ease. If you do not know what is causing the problems, how can you affect lasting change?

Heart of the Gospel

In Part 1: Laying the Foundation, we will begin by looking first at our origins. Whether we realise it consciously or not, we each hold a belief about our origins, how we humans and this earth came into existence. Something important to us is a sense of identity and purpose, and this is attached to our origins.

In Part 2: Understanding our Spiritual Nature, we will develop the origins theme further by taking a look at what makes us human, a relational being that thinks, feels, and acts.

Part 3: Disconnection discusses the consequences of unmet emotional or attachment needs, the development of mental health issues, and personality disorders, arising from a multi-layered disconnection that starts with or from God.

Finally, Part 4: The Gospel as the Cure attempts to highlight how our emotional and psychological health can be improved and restored through an understanding of the gospel.

Understanding the Heart of the Gospel and its relevance and application to the struggles of the human heart may not, at first, seem credible, especially in our modern technological and scientific-driven world. But I hope that you will see that the Gospel is timeless in its claim as being the only real hope for each of us. It costs nothing but a little faith, something you are using right now to navigate day-to-day living whether you realise it or not. Let me begin to show you how…

PART I:

Laying the Foundation

Chapter 1:

Creation vs Evolution: A Matter of Faith

The best way to understand any belief, ideology, theory, or even the storyline in a movie, is to know the genesis or beginning. Science and religion have competed to explain how life on Planet Earth started, in order to help us to comprehend why we exist, and the complexities and conflicts in human beings and the natural world around us.

There are various theories and explanations that have developed over time in attempts to provide us with an understanding of our origins, but they have contradicted themselves and caused confusion. But on closer examination, they arise solely from two ideas or views. Both require faith to believe, as no human was there at the beginning to see how the earth was formed, and how life began. We are, as it were, working backwards using the only source of evidence provided, the world around us. The two ideas or views are: (a) that this earth and its teeming lifeforms arose spontaneously from nothing, or (b) the earth and its teeming lifeforms have their origins in a creator or creators that are not of this world.

Working Backwards.

"The end is in the beginning" is a popular quote taken from the prologue in Ralph Ellison's book *The Invisible Man.* The idea that the end is somehow linked to the beginning is taken as an absolute. How can you have an end without a beginning? It is easy to conclude an end when you know the start or beginning. It starts to get trickier when we try to understand the beginning from the endpoint. This is the basic idea behind the questions about our beginnings.

Where did we come from and what (if anything) was before us?

Science and religion have the same evidence before them; the world around us and us as humans, which are the end result of something that has already happened. As I mentioned earlier, we are working backwards, trying to find the beginning from the end. And this involves faith, simply because no human was there in the beginning. Now I know there may be those reading this who will query what I mean by faith or will question this statement. Science, after all, is based on empirical evidence, which can be proven rationally using the senses. Faith is limited to the realm of religious beliefs and mythical legends.

However, religious beliefs and mythical legends use the same evidence provided to the scientist. It is interpreted differently according to what or who is believed to have created the world that we live, move, and breathe in. Both science and religion are attempting to prove their view of how both we and this world came to be. But the view or premise is a faith, and both are simply looking for evidence to support or verify the faith. No human was there at the beginning to observe and record what occurred. Science, religion, and legends all use faith to promote their conclusions.

Defining Faith.

So, what is faith? Our English understanding of faith comes from the Latin *fides* which is defined as confidence or trust in a person, thing, or concept. It is important to recognise that what we believe our origin to be influences how we regard the natural world around us that governs our lives.

Taking this definition of faith and combining this with the two main streams of thought for why and how we exist we have the following:

a) **Theory of Evolution:** If we come from nothing, then we can only have confidence in ourselves, our ideas or concepts, and our actions. And as we come from nothing, there is no real meaning for living beyond ourselves, and as our end is in the beginning, we go to nothing when we die. Or:

b) **Theory of Creation:** If there is a Creator, then there is a being who has the right to determine the meaning of our existence, and to whom we are accountable.

Dilemmas.

Both views have considerable implications and influence on how we live our lives. Viewpoint (a) brings dilemmas such as: why do we die? Where do we go when we die? Why do we love? What is morality? What is consciousness? Why do we even exist? Viewpoint (b) presents questions on the nature and character of the Creator. Why have they allowed evil to exist? Are they even involved? Why do they cause us to suffer? How do we please them? How do we get to know them?

These and other questions arise naturally from the faith view that we choose to interpret the world that we find ourselves living in. It is impossible to be alive in this world and not have, albeit subconsciously, a belief about our origins. Whether we are created or came by chance, from nothing or someone.

Faith Is a Choice.

I have chosen to believe that there is a Creator, who created this world and human beings. I have chosen to believe this viewpoint because to me it makes more sense than the scientific theories proposed. It also makes more sense in understanding the problems of good and evil, life and death, and all the moral bits in between. It has been a journey to discover which God from the differing views of God and creation stories that abound in all the different religious belief systems and legends.

My conviction is based on the revelation of God as found within the Holy Bible, a book that has for the most part been the subject of intense critiquing and criticism or consigned to the realm of fables (and this is from other religious systems, never mind the scientific arena). I do agree with some issues critically raised. The Holy Bible has been used to justify wrong or oppressive systems and has been used as a means to cause suffering and discrimination.

I would not attempt to try to counteract or disprove any statement of disbelief against the Holy Bible. I would question, however, the interpretations made or concluded. It is these misinterpretations that are the cause of contention and obscure the true character of a loving Creator God who takes responsibility for the world He has created with a purpose and intent. A Creator God who does not stand aloof from His creation but took on human form and dwelt among us. Who understands our pain and also suffers along with us while the issues of good and evil are being worked out to secure eternal righteousness and peace.

The end is in the beginning…no truer statement can be made concerning the opening chapters of the Holy Bible. The book of Genesis or Beginnings is the start of what we read in Revelations, the final book of the Holy Bible, a new heaven, and a new earth. It also reveals the problems with the human heart and how this can be solved. I hope to share with you several things I have learned, not to convince but rather to soothe and hopefully provide alternative answers to remedy the emotional and psychological pain caused by simply living in this world...

Chapter 2:

Faith: Essential Evidence in Science

In the previous chapter, I briefly discussed the two theories proposed to explain our existence. Either we are created by a Creator with intent as per creation theory, or we arise spontaneously from nothing as suggested by the theory of evolution. Both views are statements of faith as no human was there at the beginning to record and pass down what happened. Each theory uses the same evidence, this world and us, which are the results of something that has already happened.

I also shared that I believed in the theory of creation. God created this world and humans as revealed in the Holy Bible. I intend to look further at our origins from this perspective and the explanations this view offers on how our psychological and physical well-being has been affected. There is no doubt that humanity is suffering mentally, emotionally, and physically.

Two Approaches Based on Faith.

The approach we take to relieve this suffering is linked to what we believe regarding our origins. Modern medicine, including psychiatry, is founded on the principal belief of evolution. Despite this view of our origins only arising within the last few centuries, it is now the predominant worldview, even within religious countries or cultures.

This view naturally leads to the conclusion that the causes of psychological suffering, and the solutions, can only come from humans. Relieving human suffering has been the search of the great intellectuals and philosophers among us (today we call them scientists). We owe so much

Heart of the Gospel

to them for giving us an understanding of the natural or physical world on which our modern society is built.

Yet, there is still a huge mystery and that is life itself. Humans have accomplished much in understanding and even manipulating the laws of life (think of this every time you turn on your light or travel by plane), but the actual substance of life itself remains a mystery. We can only preserve or sustain what is there. Once life is gone, we cannot bring it back.

If, however, we take the view of creation, this mystery is resolved by accepting there is a God who created life. To the more rationally minded, this may seem like a leap in the darkness of ignorance, but there are times when rational thinking needs to be suspended to gain understanding.

Faith In Action.

Take, for instance, written language, using English as an example. Most people know the English Alphabet has twenty-six letters beginning with A and ending with Z. We may be able to logically learn how the alphabet letters came about, but how do we learn the phonetic sounds? How did we learn that A was A? How did we learn that it made an "ay or ah" sound? By the mechanism of simple non-questioning faith. How do we really know A is A? We do not, but we believe it to be so, and by doing so we can speak, understand, and enjoy the English language. To doubt or disbelieve that A is simply A (or any of the other letters) is to close off the ability to understand and speak the English language.

The same logic can be applied to understanding this world as being created. The famous verse, Genesis 1:1 states, "In the beginning God created the heavens and the earth." (Incidentally, the first transmitted recording of the astronauts on their first orbit around the Moon in 1968 was reading the first ten verses of Genesis 1).

By believing that we exist as a creation of God, we can start understanding the mystery of life. Life is from God and, therefore, He has the right to define the existence of life. And here is our biggest challenge. To truly accept a belief in God is to accept that we as humans are subject to a supreme being and are not as autonomous as we believe. To accept that our existence is limited by the fact that humans are restricted to the conditions for life as set by God. Phew... this can be hard to admit!

Unbelief, Our Biggest Obstacle.

If hearing these words makes you feel irritated, sceptical, angry, or wanting to shut off from reading any further, this could reveal that the first problem with the human heart or mind is disconnection from God. So great is this disconnection that humans, who according to Genesis were made in the image of God, believe that we alone determine our existence. Ask yourself honestly the question, who controls you? I am sure the answer you would give is "I do" unless I am a child or have physical or psychological restrictions that make me dependent on other humans. I am the one in charge of me! I decide my reality, my life! I wonder if this natural attitude is a cause of our stress and anxiety.

This question has as much importance to those who believe in a creator God as those who choose not to believe. I deliberately use the word *choose* as it is impossible to deny the existence of God without there being the possibility of God existing. You cannot deny anything that does not exist, even as an idea. If it is not there, it is not there, period.

For many today, there is the idea of God, but only as a mental construct that humans used in the past to ascribe phenomena that can now be explained by science. But this idea of there being a God is so outdated, it is now considered a belief of primitive man.

Heart of the Gospel

But ideas exist, don't they? To say ideas or concepts do not exist is to flatly deny human invention and development. Everything humans have made or developed, first started as an idea or image before being brought into physical actuality, where it can be appreciated by the senses of sight, hearing, touch, taste, and smell. Even ideologies do this. Think about the ideologies of capitalism and socialism and how they are affecting your actual finances.

Faith in God Simplifies

The acceptance of there being a creator God is by the same mechanism that we accept and learn the English alphabet, by simple faith. Accepting the letters of the alphabet as just being and sounding as they are, unlocks the mysteries of the English (or any) language and enjoys its benefits. To do otherwise would deconstruct the English language, wasting a lot of time, energy, and resources in the process. By accepting God as the creator, we can understand our world and ourselves. What we learn initially may challenge us, but it can provide a start to answering the big questions of who we are, where we came from, and most importantly, where we are going. But all these answers rest on the premise of faith.

For without faith, it is impossible. Those who come to God must first believe that He exists.

Chapter 3:

Nature of Man: Part Spirit, Part Physical

So far, I have attempted to lay a foundation based on faith in the creation of this world and humans by a personal Creator God as opposed to the other faith view, the spontaneous development from nothing as proposed by the theory of evolution. I also intimated that what we believe our origins to be, influences how we see ourselves, live our lives, and attempt to solve the many difficulties we face.

Modern medicine, including psychiatry, is firmly entrenched in the theory of evolution and therefore concludes that human beings are only biological or physical beings, who evolved through a series of complex steps over time. The ability to have thoughts and emotions are the result of biological processes, and electrical impulses, which have somehow been encoded genetically and passed down through reproduction.

With the development of imaging in neuroscience, we can see the molecular movements occurring in the brain when a person is thinking a thought or feeling an emotion. But what is causing the molecular movements or electrical impulses observed? Is it just random biological processing? Or could it be that what is being observed through neuroimaging are the physical signs in the brain of something else?

God Is a Spirit Being

Evolution naturally excludes the belief that God created man in His image, after His likeness. As a result, the possibility that man is also a spirit being is dismissed, not even considered. Modern medicine and psychiatry unintentionally conclude that man is just a one-sided physical being and therefore focus solely on this aspect. The Bible adds another layer. In John 4:24, the nature of God is revealed. "God is a Spirit, and they that worship Him must worship in spirit and in truth."

This does not mean that God is some ethereal being that has no substance, but rather the essence of God, which is Spirit, is different from the material nature or quality of the visible world created. In making man or humans after His image and likeness, God has created us as dual-natured beings. To explain this, we need to go back to the creation of man as revealed in Genesis chapters 1 and 2.

Man has a Spirit

In the first chapter of Genesis, we read how God created the heavens and the earth and all life forms by His Word. The material universe, heavens and earth were spoken into reality by the Word of God. The heavens and earth that we know were not originally made from the natural elements we can see and touch. They were spoken into existence by God, whose nature does not consist of the things made. To every living thing formed, God gave the ability to reproduce itself: plants, animals, and humans.

In making humans, God did something extra. In Genesis 1:26, we read God stating, "Let us make Man in our image, after our likeness, and let them have dominion over all the other life forms on earth." In Verse 27 it continues that God made Man in His image (singular); male and female, He made them (plural).

Genesis 2:7 reveals that Man was created in a unique way that sets him apart from the rest of creation. Here, we read how God formed man from the dust of the earth and breathed directly into his nostrils the breath of life. It is important to understand that the earth or dust contained life, as God had spoken the earth into existence. We know scientifically today that the earth or soil is a living substance. Being a living thing, the earth itself just needed

Heart of the Gospel

to be moulded into whatever form desired, whether it be trees, plants, or animals. The same life-giving element was in the waters which brought forth the sea creatures and birds, as God commanded.

Only into man, however, did God breathe directly, imparting to man His Spiritual nature. Man is a dual being made from both the natural earth over which he was to rule and the spirit that enables man to commune and relate to God as a spiritual being. Humans are the link species between the natural and spiritual realms or dimensions that make up heaven and earth. We are similar and yet completely different from the rest of the animal kingdom. If you are wondering at this point what is meant by spiritual realms or dimensions, I am talking about what is beyond the physical. Take, for instance, the nature of air or the wind. We know scientifically these substances exist as we can feel or hear wind and air. But we cannot see, hold or contain them. Just like the heavens or sky, they are part of the spiritual realm that surrounds us.

We were formed physically from the same substance as other animals, but we are miles apart in function and capabilities and the only creature that has a moral conscience. We are created in the image and likeness of God with a spirit. This is a profound reality on which the true value and worth of each human being rests, but an image or likeness is not the actual thing. It is just an outline or reflection.

The image of yourself you see reflected in the mirror is not you in person. So, in the creation of Man, God created humans with the capacity to reflect the image and likeness of God as a living mirror, but **NOT** be God themselves. Even more than just being a glorified mirror, the image of God in man was to be maintained by an intimate relationship with each of us being a willing participant. This is where the concept of man having free will, and the ability to choose originates. Humans were originally designed to reflect the image of the God who created them by giving humans a mind or spirit.

Brain vs Mind

The human brain may be the most complex structure known in the world and yet this brain is just part of our physical or natural body. The brain, however, is not the mind but rather acts as the essential vehicle through which the mind can find expression. We can see and dissect the brain. We cannot see or dissect the mind.

If you were asked the question, what is the mind? – what answer would you give? How do we know we even have a mind? Well, we know we have a mind because we think, feel, and behave. But are our thoughts, feelings, and behaviours just biological processes? Or are they manifestations of us as spirit beings, our minds being a part of our spiritual nature?

We are familiar with the titles of psychology, psychiatry, psychotherapy, psychoanalysis etc, relating to all things to do with our mental health and well-being. Many of us have a counsellor or therapist to support us in managing our "minds." I happen to be one of these and feel privileged to be able to support others. But do we understand what these titles mean? The common root prefix in all these words comes from the Greek *psyche* or *psykhe* which is defined as ***"the soul, mind, spirit, or invisible animating entity which occupies the physical body."*** Did you get that? So, when you go to the doctors for support for anxiety or depression, and they refer you to any of the above professionals listed, you are seeking support for the spiritual, not the physical side of you!

Why We Have Thoughts and Words.

I would like to give you something else to consider as this section closes. I briefly discussed the creation view of how

God created this world with His Word. God made Man in His image and likeness as a spiritual being. As humans we all have thoughts inside our minds, but how are our thoughts made known to others? How do we share our inner thoughts and feelings? We express our thoughts by speaking words in either verbal or written form. Our thoughts have to be made visible or known somehow for us to be understood.

Our thoughts or words are not physical. You cannot grab or hold them with your hands or examine them under a microscope, but they are very real. They are non-material, or spiritual, the revelations of you as a spirit being in a way that can be physically known. This is communication, the basis of social relationships. There are so many facets to us as spiritual beings. Our ability to think, reason, imagine, create, decide and so much more makes us human because we are spirit beings. Evolution cannot fully account for the marked differences between humans and animals, but creation theory can. We are made in the image of God.

PART 2:

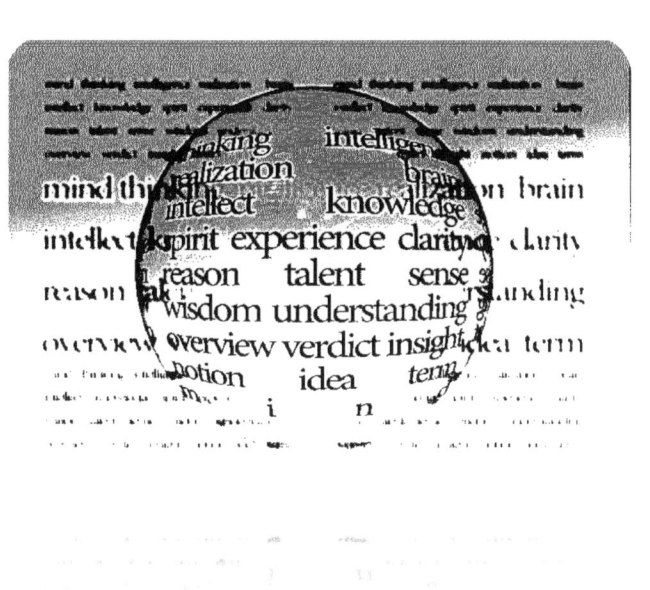

Understanding our Spiritual Nature

Chapter 1:

Beginnings

Part One laid a foundation for the biblical view of the creation and nature of humans. The concept of humans being dual-natured, having both a physical and non-physical aspect, was alluded to briefly. I hope to elaborate this further in this chapter, to make it clear what our spiritual nature looks like. If you cannot describe what part of you is hurting, e.g., your leg or hand, it is certain the cause of your pain will be wrongly diagnosed. There will be some references to the biblical book of Genesis in this chapter. Please bear with me on this as it is necessary. It may be helpful to have a read of Genesis chapters one and two if you are unfamiliar with this account or version of creation.

Genesis 1 gives us a grand overview of how God, through His Word, created the heavens, the earth, and every living thing in six days and rested on the seventh. Did you know that there is no marker for a seven-day week found in nature? The day can be measured by how long it takes the earth to rotate on its axis. The month can be calculated by the phases of the moon. The year is calculated by the orbiting of the sun around the earth, but there is no natural event for the weekly cycle. Civilizations in the past have attempted to shorten or lengthen the week without success. Something inherent keeps the week as a seven-day cycle.

A Closer Look at The Creation of Man

According to the sequence found in Genesis 1, human beings appear to have been made on the sixth day. This is what is commonly believed and taught. However, I would like to propose that the male was made on the third day and completed with the female on the sixth day. This view is contrary to the normal understanding, but let me explain. Chapter Two of Genesis focuses on the actual making of human beings. Verse 7 of this chapter informs us that God formed man (physical) from the dust of the ground and breathed into his nostrils (spiritual) and man became a living soul. The totality of who we are is called a soul, consisting of both a physical body and a spiritual nature that animates or gives life to the physical. You and I, according to the Bible, are souls.

Verses 4-6 inform us that this event occurred when there was no vegetation yet on the earth. If we contrast this with the overview sequencing given in Chapter One, we can see this was around the third day. God then proceeded to plant a garden in the east of Eden and placed the newly formed man there, before calling forth vegetation on the earth. It is not until further along in the chapter, after the making of the animals, does the creation of the female happen. If we again simply contrast this event with the order of creation as given in chapter one, we come to the sixth day. Male and female humans were not created on the same day, or at the same time. We are distinct from each other, and we are binary in origin.

Human Beings Created With Purpose:

Genesis 1 26-27 reveals God's purposes for creating humans. Apart from being in the likeness and image of the Creator, we were created to occupy a position of dominion and control over the earth. We were created as relational beings, to be in relationships. We were created to subdue the earth, to reproduce and fill the earth with more humans, reflecting the image and likeness of God. This earth was created to be our home territory. Even now, as humans, we seek to be or desire to be masters over our own lives and affairs. The lack or inability to have mastery is a primary cause of mental distress. It is innately built into us.

Heart of the Gospel

To have dominion or rulership over the earth is a huge undertaking. However, God equipped humans in His design of us to do just this. Going back again to Genesis 2, we can discuss this further. The first step God takes after making a man is planting a garden for him in Eden. The description and location of Eden appear to be the place where the spiritual realm directly connected to the physical earth. Eden is symbolic of the presence of God, who is Spirit. A garden or dwelling place for man was prepared. The man was given the duty to dress (serve, work) and keep (protect) the garden.

As soon as the male was created, he was put to the service of work. Please do not underestimate the importance to males of having an occupation and being put in a position of responsibility. It is an integral part of the male psyche to be able to work, serve, and protect. This is what his body is built for and his mind or spirit. You can see how unemployment in particular affects males more deeply than females. The male mind, in particular, sees things in more concrete and absolute terms and can be more logical and decisive because of this purpose. The man was given the earth as his dominion, his territory to rule over, but this could only happen if man were himself subject to boundaries.

Human Beings are not Limitless

You may have heard the phrase "absolute power corrupts absolutely." To have total power or liberty to do whatever you want without consideration of the needs of others or consequences would create a despot. It would also create a being that cannot relate or be in a relationship with any other apart from itself. Having given man the full reign over the earth and lower life forms, God places man under restriction. He limits His access to everything. There is one tree man is forbidden to eat the fruit of.

Now, I do not intend to go into the debates about what type of fruit this is or whether this is to be taken literally or figuratively. No matter what we believe faith-wise, I am sure we have heard the story of how humans fell by eating from the Tree of Knowledge after being tempted by the serpent or snake. The point I am making here is that Man was given a boundary.

Boundaries are important for safety, self-control, and proper functioning. Throughout creation, God set boundaries everywhere. He separated the light from the darkness. The sky above from the waters underneath. The earth was divided from the waters to create land. Birds fly in the air, fish swim in the sea, and the stars orbit the heavens. Boundaries are necessary for humans to fulfil the purpose of their creation. Obedience to those boundaries keeps humans alive.

Humans are under Moral Boundaries

No other animal on this planet functions from a moral base, only humans. Having made man after His image and likeness, God placed man in an environment that reflected His nature. An environment where everything was good. An environment where everything was based on the principle of love. God is love. And if you know anything about the principle of love, you will appreciate that love does not compel, love does not force. Humans were granted the option to agree with the conditions of life by obeying the one restriction placed on them. This was the role of the Tree of Knowledge.

Although humans are the marvel point of creation and given dominion over the earth, they are not autonomous. The dominion and authority given over the earth is subordinate to the submission of the human to the Creator. Humans reflect the image and likeness of God. An image or likeness is of no use without its substance or source. As God is love, He has given Man the ability to love and reflect that

Heart of the Gospel

love, by giving the precious gift of choice, free will. To make humans any other way would be to make robots, incapable of relating and developing.

Freedom to choose is not the "do as you want" attitude believed today. Free will is the decision or choice to agree with the conditions, to enjoy life as set by the Creator. It places an obligation to remind Man that his life and abilities are under the authority of One that is higher. It was a simple instruction. "Do not eat from the Tree of Knowledge. If you do, you will forfeit the conditions of life by choosing to die." No further information or knowledge was given regarding death. The man had to accept by faith the Word spoken and choose to obey the instruction. Moral behaviour requires the ability to choose. Today, we are conflicted with right and wrong, good and evil because of the choice to disobey. We will discuss this in more detail in later chapters.

Chapter 2:

Understanding the Male and the Female

So far, we have been discussing the creation of Man as the male. The female has not yet been brought onto the scene as we continue in Genesis 2. We have briefly discussed the purpose for human creation, to reflect the image and likeness of God (in short, His personality or character), to have dominion over the earth, and be in a relationship. Another aspect of the purpose is to reproduce and fill the earth with more humans and subdue or manage the lower life forms of animals and vegetation. Nowhere in this mandate is it given for a human to have dominion or rulership over another human!

So far, in Genesis 1 and 2, we see God relating one-on-one with the male human, and giving him his assignment and responsibilities of serving and protecting. The male was given the choice and ability to agree with the conditions for life, to obey and to be in submission. I am deliberately referring to or making the distinction of the "male human" here because I am building a premise that I hope you will understand shortly about our spiritual nature.

After creating the male and setting him up in position, God brings into view the next purpose of creating humans: relationships. In Genesis 2:18, God makes an interesting statement. God declares that it is ***not*** good for the male to be alone. A mate, a companion to be with, and support are required. It is important to understand that the male bore the image and likeness of God entirely on his own. The female was not made to complete the image or likeness of God. Both the male and the female in themselves are reflective of the image of God.

Testing the Cognitive Faculties

Just before making the female, God brings to the man all the animals for him to name. This is not as simple as it sounds. To give something a name means describing its purpose, function, or capabilities. It also implies the taking of ownership or responsibility for the thing named. The latter speaks volumes as to why we name our pets. The man was given this task by God, potentially as a testing of the cognitive, rational parts of his spirit. To see if this functions similarly to His own.

It also could be the means of showing the male his own need for someone to relate to. In seeing the animals in groups, he would realise that he was in the singular. Remember, man is the link species between the spiritual and physical realms. Animals could only relate to him so far as they do not possess a rational spirit and are subject mainly to physical laws. Enabling the male to see his need for a companion through this process may have been the intent to gain the man's consent for the next bit, to give up a part of his body. After all, God is love, and love never compels.

The Making of the Female:

In making the female, God was even more unique in His method than with the male. Here is the first recorded operation. In Genesis 2:21-22, we read how after putting the male into a deep sleep, God took a rib from his side and made the female. I like how in the Hebrew language it translates that God *built* the female. After forming and fashioning the female, God brought her to the male.

Today, in our world, there is so much division and strife over the differences in gender advantages and roles. In the sight of God, males and females are equivalent in value and worth. The female was made from the rib, taken out of the physical side of man as an equal. Not to rule or dominate over the male or be trodden underfoot by him, but to work side by side in fulfilling the purpose of their creation. The only differences were in the roles they had to fulfil.

The female was taken out of the male. This is an important principle not based on biological sex or gender, but on position order. The male came before the female just as God comes before the male. All the qualities of the female were within the male initially. God separated or distributed certain aspects of Himself between the male and female for relationship and functioning. Between them both they have dominion over the earth.

God took a rib from the male's body, symbolizing the softer, sensory nature of the female, as being more intuitive than rational. This is a known, marked difference between males and females. Both are essential for functioning. We need both the rational and intuitive to weigh up any situation. But God ordained that it is the rational part that makes the final decision or choice. The instruction not to eat from the Tree of Knowledge was given to the male without the female being present.

Further on in the chapter, we learn that it is the male that names the female "woman," again cementing the fact that the male in this respect has the pre-eminence. The female came out of the male. By naming the female, the male takes responsibility for serving and protecting her. In her capacity, the female creates the ability for a male to relate to and love another as himself.

A Composite of Both Male and Female

I hope I have not totally confused your understanding, but to make sure that what I am trying to say is clear, here is a quick recap. God made humans to have dominion over the earth and subdue or keep under control the lower life forms and vegetation. We were made to reflect the image and likeness of God through relationships. God initially made the male human first and assigned to him his particular duties and responsibilities: to serve, protect, and hold accountability. To fulfil the purpose of relationships, God created the female from the male to assist him and relate to him.

By distributing His divine attributes between both the male and the female, the Image and likeness of God is replicated. Each has accountability before Him to remain in the roles designated. This does not mean, and should not be taken as, a view endorsing females as not being rational. We are! We are spirit beings and being rational is part of our spiritual nature. We just tend to be more on the intuitive side than males, picking up more information on a sensory, non-verbal level than males, and having more of a "right gut instinct." This ability makes females more nurturing and relational, which prepares them for the primary role of being mothers, as part of reproduction.

There is also another reason it is important to understand the differences between the male and the female as it relates to us. Each of us, whether biologically male or female, is a mixture of both. We each have a rational cognitive side and an emotional sensory side on both the spiritual and physical levels. Our physical bodies contain both the primary male and female hormones, testosterone, and oestrogen. The levels of each are determined primarily by the gene expression of the X or Y chromosome we are randomly assigned at conception. Males have some oestrogen; females have some testosterone. It is well known that imbalances in hormone levels or functions can cause multiple physical and psychological issues.

Two Sides to our Brains

The brain itself is semi-divided into two hemispheres. The left hemisphere functions tend to be more analytical and logical. The left side processes verbal language and factual, sequential information. The right hemisphere functions are more creative, imaginative, and intuitive. The right side processes non-verbal language, spatial awareness, and intuition. We have implicit and explicit memory that governs all the various ways we remember, store, and recall information. Each side working together is necessary for us to function – the masculine side of rationality, fact, and explicitness combined with the creative, intuitive, and implicit feminine side.

I hope you are beginning to understand why it is important to understand the differences between males and females as ordained by God. Not just as different genders externally, but also how our spiritual nature is made up internally. There is a principle in Theology and other philosophical studies known as repetition and enlargement. Something within a small scale is replicated on a larger scale. Or something internal is made external. This principle is used to gradually bring to view the bigger picture of what is contained in the miniature.

God ordained for the male human to serve and protect the female externally. The female is appointed to accept the divine order and work alongside the male. Likewise, the logical, rational side of our spirit is to serve and protect the emotional side internally. The emotional side is to accept and conform to the decisions made by the rational side. A reversing of this order, where the emotions dominate the rational, is at the heart of many mental health disorders we experience today.

Chapter 3:

Attachment: Why We Need It

In contemplating the purposes for which God created human beings, I hope you are beginning to have a growing appreciation of yourself as a unique person of worth simply because you are formed in the image of God. You have a starting point that is above your earthly family of origin. You are not the result of a random biological process that took aeons to develop you into the human you are. There is a place for you in the grand scheme of things as a descendant of Adam (Adam is the generic Hebrew term for humans, both male and female).

The last chapter focused on exploring the creation and roles of males and females as both externally separate beings, as well as representations of internal parts of our spirit. The rational side or functions are linked to the male while the emotional/sensory side or functions are linked to the female. Both are necessary and equally valid. But God ordained that the male or rational side takes the lead and makes the final decision. It is as if we have two separate brains that need to work together in unison. This often requires one to make the final decision. God determined it would be the male or rational side.

Connection To the Source of Life

So, although man was created to have dominion and rulership over the earth, he was not created to do this as an autonomous being. Humans were given the ability to agree, to consent to the conditions that would enable this life and position to continue. As complex and capable as the human mind or spirit is, it was not designed to operate without being under the influence or guidance of another mind or spirit. We were developed to reflect the image and likeness of God, His personality. To do this, we must be in connection with His mind or spirit.

If we recall the creation of the male, we remember that he was made first and placed in a garden in Eden, where an instruction was given to him not to eat from the tree of The Knowledge of Good and Evil or else he would die. In this command, three things are established. The first is that Man has been created with the ability to choose, or with free will. The second is that by giving the command not to do something, the possibility of that very thing being done is generated. The third is that continued life is dependent on obedience to the command. Humans were created mortal, not immortal.

Through this one limitation and warning placed on Man, God set the conditions for how life was to continue. The requirement is a connection to Him through faith and obedience. By choosing to comply, the man was able to remain in the presence of God, be joined to Him in his spirit, and continue to live. Adam had no knowledge or idea at this point what death meant. It was just something they were warned would happen if they chose otherwise. Faith has been and always will be a part of living and being alive. We use faith every day. We do not know the consequences or outcome of every instruction we receive. We just accept and abide by them and so far, we have done okay. We put our faith in human words all the time, but we struggle to put faith in God's Word. How ironic is that? There is a reason we naturally doubt it. I will come back to this point in the next section.

Attachment Necessary to Fulfil Divine Purpose:

I know I keep repeating that humans were made in the image of God, to reflect His likeness, but this is so important. The Bible tells us that God is love. God is the very essence of love, and He created man with the ability to

Heart of the Gospel

relate to and reflect His nature of love. Today, Hollywood and novels teach us to see love as a powerful emotional state rather than an act of will or decision. We are encouraged to look for some kind of euphoria or deep sensory knowing that this person is the one. Unfortunately, our emotions, like the sea, also ebb and flow or even fizzle out. When this happens, we conclude that we have fallen out of love.

The love of God is a constant power that has its source beyond the physical or material world we live in. Love is far more than an emotion or feeling. It is the abiding law or principle of life that all living things need. Furthermore, humans are purposed to reflect this love. To facilitate this, God built laws within our minds, and emotional needs to be met primarily in our relationship with Him and to be shared and developed with other humans. Just as all the colours of the rainbow are combined within white light, separating as it passes through a prism, we can attempt to break love down into strands or components.

They are **Acceptance, Affirmation, Attention, Affection, Guidance, Discipline, Protection, and Comfort**. Psychologists have many ways of describing our emotional or attachment needs, but they usually include these eight. These needs are hardwired into our emotional spiritual nature and are more than what can be humanly supplied alone. God designed them to be met primarily in attachment to Him by the rational decision to accept His Word and obey, by faith.

These emotional needs work in partnership with the laws of the mind to also aid in the purpose that God created us for, to reflect and develop more fully His divine nature of love. So, what are some of these laws of the mind?

1. The law of beholding and adaptation (2 Corinthians 3: 18). Today this is known in neuropsychology as "mirroring." We have mirror neuron networks in our brains that enable us to not only learn through observation but emotionally participate in what we

observe. This law also gives us the ability to form mental images and retain them.
2. The Law of Conviction (Proverbs 23:7). What we believe and feel motivates our behaviour.
3. The law of hope/desire (Psalms 22:9). Hope is the desire or expectation of something happening, by trusting someone to make it happen. Even if that someone is yourself. Depression always contains the loss of hope or trust in ever attaining what we desire. The greater the hopelessness, the deeper the depression. It is a law of our mind to hope, to desire.
4. The Law of reproduction and heredity (Genesis 5:1-3). God created humans with the ability to not only reproduce their physical nature but also the spiritual. To reproduce beings in whom His Spirit could abide so they also reflected His image and likeness. The human drive for self-preservation is linked to this law.

Only God can Completely Meet our Emotional Needs:

These and other laws of the mind, also emotional needs, were designed to be met primarily by the God who created them. No human being can completely supply these needs to another human. We can share what we have, but we cannot supply the fullness that the human heart needs. This is better understood by the two great commandments, ***"Thou shalt love the Lord thy God with all your heart, with all your soul, and with all your mind and with all your strength: this is the first commandment. And the second is like this, thou shalt love your neighbour as yourself'*** Mark 12: 29-31.

By putting God first, we place ourselves in the position to receive His presence and be supplied with our emotional and psychological needs. In knowing God, we can gain a better understanding of who we are, and instead of seeking for ourselves from others, we can love them equally. Love for God and love for each other are the two principles of the law of love which governs all the created universe. The continuous breaking of this law of love is the real cause of the evil and confusion that is in the world today.

Chapter 4:

Taking a Quick Look at our Physical Nature.

I hope it is becoming clearer what our spiritual nature or spirit is. There does tend to be a lot of mysticism around this subject that can leave us wondering what the human spirit is. I hope you now know that a spirit is you as a thinking, feeling, and behaving entity contained inside a physical, tangible body. Human beings are dual-natured by design.

Every part of our being has been created by God and placed under laws that govern how they function to complete the purpose for our creation, which was to reflect the image and likeness of God, to rule over (dominate) and manage the physical or material earth and take care of the lower orders of animals and vegetation and reproduce. To do the latter parts, we have been given a physical body, made initially from the same elements as the earth. Humans are the link species between the spiritual and physical realms that make up this planet.

While humans stayed in obedience, they remained in the presence of God as symbolized by being placed in Eden. God is a Spirit. He does not reside in the created world, but sustains His creation from the outside. God does not live in nature as some pantheistic beliefs suggest. Nature reflects and reveals the fact that there is a Creator. God purposed that His dwelling place on earth was to be within the human spirit.

The Physical Nature:

Just to recap, Genesis 1 26-27 states that God first made a male human in His image and likeness before forming his female counterpart. In Genesis chapter two verse seven, we read how God formed the male Adam from the dust of the ground and breathed into his nostrils the breath of life and man became a living soul. The word translated to English as *soul* from the Hebrew language here is *nephesh,* which means 'a breathing creature'. This is the same word that is translated as 'creature' in Genesis 1: 24, when God created the land animals.

So, here we can see some agreement with evolution. Humans do have similar characteristics as other animals, but we did not evolve or descend from lower forms. Humans (or Adam) were created with a physical or material body comparable to the land animals as part of his divine mandate to rule over the earth, but God also created humans with a spirit, to be made in His image and likeness. God breathed into the male the breath of life, or *neshama*, translated from Hebrew as the "divine inspiration or intellect." Humans were created to reflect God and thus are given a mind or spirit which at this point was in submission and accordance with God.

The human brain is one of the most fascinating and complex structures known and it has dual functions. The brain provides the link connection between our physical and spiritual natures, our minds, and our emotions. It is via the brain that we gather information from our environment, and find expression via our thoughts, words, emotions, and behaviours. The brain supports in co-ordinating and performing physical activities including sustaining life.

The brain is part of our physical body, which is a sophisticated combustion machine, using glucose, fats, and oxygen, as the main sources of energy. The food we eat, no matter how fabulously made and tasty, gets broken down into these and other basic elements to supply energy and repair. The physical body has inherent drives built into its design necessary for functioning. These drives include appetite, thirst, reproduction, threat/self- preservation, bonding, acquiring and learning.

A Simple Model of The Brain:

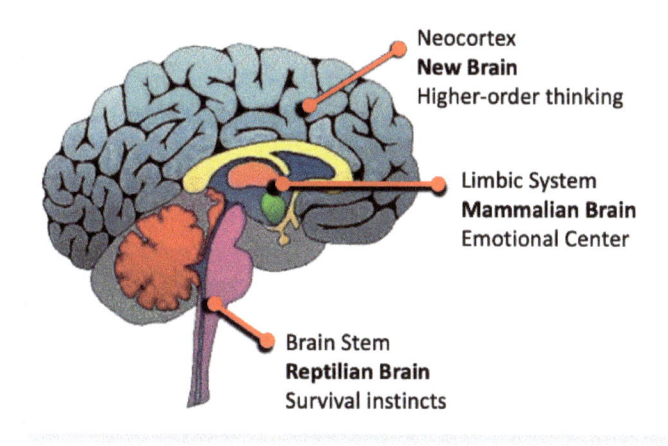

P. D. MacLean, The triune brain in evolution. New York: Plenum Press, 1990

The above illustrated model of the brain simplifies how the various parts of our brain are structured and how we process information. We have one brain that can be divided loosely into three main areas consisting of A) Brain Stem: the area that controls all our bodily functions for survival; B) Limbic System: the area that coordinates emotional/sensory processing and attachment/bonding and C) Neocortex: the area that co-ordinates rational/logical processing and decision-making.

The Limbic System.

The limbic system is the term given to the structures in the brain that together regulate our inherent drives. They are the amygdala, hippocampus, hypothalamus, thalamus, and pituitary gland.

The amygdala is known as the mental alarm bell, as it senses threats and instigates biological changes to prepare us to meet threats and preserve our lives. The hippocampus processes our memories and plays a role in learning. The hypothalamus regulates our appetites for food, thirst and sex, and communicates with the pituitary gland in secreting hormones. The thalamus is the central processing centre for all the information gathered by our physical senses and relays it to the neocortex.

The Neocortex

The human body, with its inherent drives, was placed under the higher laws of the human mind, which operates from the neocortex layer of the brain. The neocortex is made up of five main lobes or areas (frontal, occipital, parietal, temporal and insula), each having specific and overlapping tasks. The neocortex is the centre for higher brain activities such as reasoning, perception, decision-making, language, imagining, and social interaction. Most of these activities take place in the largest of the lobes, the frontal lobes.

The frontal lobes are responsible for inhibiting or controlling our inherent biological drives and are the last area of the brain to fully mature. It is most probable that the frontal lobes are where our physical and spiritual nature coincides or merges. It is with this part of our brain that we can understand and submit to higher moral laws. Animals follow the law of natural drives that regulate bodily function. The higher order of animals may have the ability to connect and engage in social interactions, but they do this instinctively, not through choice. Animals do not have a moral conscience. They cannot understand or engage with moral laws. Animals do not have the ability or capacity to reflect the divine Image.

Human Reproduction placed under Moral Law

God created a world and environment in which all these natural drives were able to be satisfied. An abundance of free food and pure water to satisfy the appetite. Pure vitalized air for oxygen, consistent temperature, and day/night cycles to support and supply the needs of the physical body. All living things, including humans, were given the divine mandate to reproduce themselves and the laws were set to govern this aspect. Humans, however, being placed under moral law, were subjected to a higher understanding of reproduction.

Human reproduction was to be more than an instinct. Remember that humans were created to reflect the divine nature of love. Human reproduction was placed under tighter boundaries than lower animals. God created males and females to relate to each other and form close connections. Human beings were given the ultimate privilege of being able to reproduce the image of God in their children; an ability and honour that was to be sacredly guarded. Marriage, a union of one woman to one man, was instituted right at the beginning.

Wherever human culture and societies have been founded, marriage relations have been a central feature. Throughout antiquity, every civilisation has developed family groupings based on this theme. Even evolution theorists, in their illustrations, have depicted pre-modern humans living in family groups with male and female partners!

Chapter 5:

We are Relational Beings

In summary of the previous chapters, I discussed how God created humans as relational beings, needing to attach, and be relationally involved to fulfil His purpose in man, which is to reflect His divine image of love. I briefly introduced the spiritual law of love that sustains all of creation and how our spiritual nature was designed to comply with this law through connection with God and with each other.

I also briefly touched on some of the laws of the mind and the emotional needs that are hardwired in us. I intend to spend more time in this chapter looking further at these emotional needs and laws of the mind. For simplicity, the term "law" is defined as the principle that governs or directs a process or action e.g., the law of gravity ensures that everything solid stays on the ground. So, what goes up must also come down.

God is a Personal Being.

Likewise, there are laws that govern or direct our mental and emotional systems. God designed these laws to enable communication and to serve Him within the context of a relationship. Now, this implies a two-way process, which goes against the normal picture presented of God as a being who demands to be worshipped with no thought or care for His subjects.

On the contrary, God created humans with all their rational and emotional capabilities to be in a relationship with Himself first and then with others. A relationship is akin to attachment and connection through the means of knowing. You know nothing about a stranger, but much about a friend. By getting to know our friends, who once were strangers, we became attached to them. Throughout the created world and within the differences between male and female, God placed the knowledge of Himself, to be understood both experientially and in a practical way.

Recap Of Emotional Needs and Spiritual Laws of The Mind.

The laws of the mind mentioned previously are:
1. **The law of beholding and adaptation** (2 Corinthians 3: 18). Today this is known in neuropsychology as "mirroring." We have mirror neurons that enable us to not only learn through observation, but emotionally participate in what we observe. This law also enables us to be empathic, and to understand the experience of others, both cognitively and emotionally. This law also facilitates our ability to adapt mentally to our environment.
2. **The Law of Conviction** (Proverbs 23:7). What we believe and think determines how we behave. This is the premise of cognitive therapy approaches. By changing our beliefs and thoughts, we can improve our emotions and change our behaviours for the better.
3. **The law of hope and trust** (Psalms 22:9). The ability to hope and trust is essential to positive mental health. God created us to hope and desire Him primarily. This law governs our need for bonding and intimacy with others and ourselves.
4. **The Law of heredity** (Genesis 5: 1-3). God created humans with the ability to reproduce both their physical and spiritual natures. The physical drives to acquire, reproduce, and preserve self are linked to this.

If Adam had obeyed by faith the command God gave them, these and other psychological laws would operate perfectly

in maintaining a relationship with God. Humanity would continue to dwell within the presence of God, having all our emotional (love) needs met. These needs can be broken down as:
1. The need for acceptance; to be welcomed, be a part of, belonging
2. The need for affirmation; to be valued, respected
3. The need for attention; to be focused on, listened to
4. The need for affection; given the sense that you are loved
5. The need for guidance; to be given and helped toward a future
6. The need for discipline; to be instructed, mentored by example
7. The need for protection; to feel secure, safe
8. The need for comfort; a reduced sense of want

Protection is a primal emotional need. Out of all the creatures in this world, Man has the least ability to protect himself. We have no horns, no claws, no scales, etc., to defend ourselves against the other creatures, yet he was to rule over them. Full dominion could only occur in connection with God, in submission to the divine command. Today, it is well documented that stress and anxiety are the main causes of both physical and mental ill health in humanity. The human threat response is over-stimulated by the perceived threats lurking everywhere. Despite all our efforts to make ourselves safe, we still feel unprotected, physically, emotionally, and mentally.

Emotional Needs Differ Between Males and Females.

These emotional needs are essential to both males and females but are expressed differently. Females have a greater need for intimacy primarily because of their role as nurturers. Females are more responsive and intuitive. None of these qualities lessen female intelligence, but they can

Heart of the Gospel

and do influence how this intelligence is demonstrated. Females are known to be able to see the "bigger picture" better than males, who tend to be more focused and logical, relying more on reason than intuition.

Males tend to initiate and regulate systems and order. It is no coincidence that occupations that require systematic thinking such as science, technology, and mathematics are predominantly male. I am not intimating in any way that females cannot excel in these areas. We have many female contributions in these areas to prove this is not so. However, it is often overlooked that lots of females choose not to enter these areas, not just because of the lack of opportunities afforded them, but also because of the reduced emotional and social connections these types of professions give.

Males usually want to know the reason "why" about things. It is probable that needing to see the reason why affects the success of males in the educational system. If the reason for learning x, y, or z cannot be understood, then what is the point? The male brain zones out. Male children tend to be more inquisitive and explorative than females, but our modern school system does not cater adequately for this distinction. Boys are more likely to be labelled disruptive when the cause in most cases is simply boredom.

Females generally have a need to be connected to one another, which is supported by the creation point of view. They were never created alone. God created the male first and stated it was not good for him to be alone. God made woman for Man to love, to share the love God gave him to another, to watch over and protect. By loving another, a man loves himself.

A female finds her ultimate fulfilment in nurturing others, in building up other humans. I know this goes against the grain of what we are taught as females today. But we also see the reality of many women who have spent years nurturing and building their own businesses and careers, sadly admitting in the latter years of their lives, that they have not been fulfilled in any of their achievements unless it involved the development and mentoring of other people. Many such females regret not having children or stable, intimate relationships.

As we come to the end of **Section 2: Understanding our Spiritual Nature**, I hope there has been a further understanding of your human spirit. I have spent some time focusing on the creation and differences between males and females for a reason. Each of us is a product of a male and female union and is born either male or female, unless an error in cell division or mutations occur and a baby is born intersex, having both genitalia. And yet, even in these rare cases, if the child is left alone, a natural inclination to be male or female becomes obvious. The wonderful Lady Colin Campbell springs to mind as a living example!

A Final Thought.

Genesis 5:1-3 informs us that humans, who were originally created in the likeness and image of God, are now reproducing our own image and likeness. Because of the fall (the umbrella term used regarding Adam's choice to disobey God), humans have inherited and pass on certain genetic traits that negatively affect our emotional and psychological well-being to varying degrees. We now inherit a spiritual nature that is disconnected from God, and no longer in submission to Him. So, what does this nature look like? This is what we will examine in the next section.

PART 3:

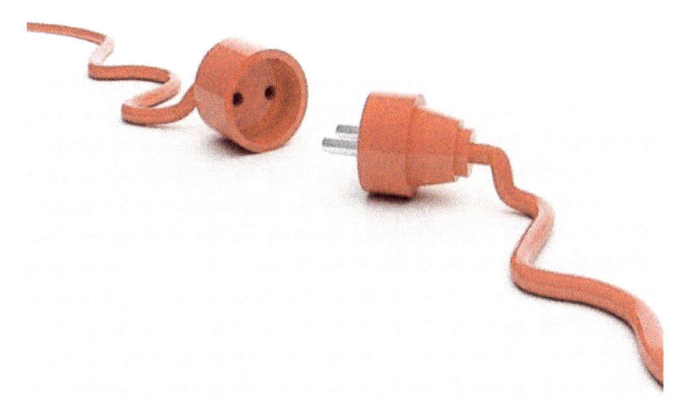

This Photo by Unknown Author is licensed under CC

Disconnected

Chapter 1:

The Emotional and Psychological Effects of Disconnection

The previous section focused on the unique dual nature of human beings, who were originally created in the divine image and likeness of God. We are equipped with an ability to connect and relate to God through our spiritual nature and be in connection with the material earth through our physical nature. We spent some time reviewing how our emotional and psychological faculties were designed to enable humans to be relational beings, communicating with God, with other humans, and with our individual selves. We all have essential emotional needs, hardwired into our minds, which must be met according to the law or function of our spiritual nature. We were created to love and be loved, to have our emotional needs met primarily by God and to be shared or mirrored with others.

Unmet Emotional Needs.

The social, medical, educational, and judicial systems all acknowledge unmet emotional needs as the primary source for the various negative life outcomes experienced. Adverse childhood experiences, or ACES, are a well-used predictor for the likelihood that someone will experience poor health, social, and overall life functioning. The more adverse events endured during childhood, the higher the risk of developing a serious physical or mental health issue in adulthood. The risk also climbs for entering the judicial system, failing school, instability in employment, substance misuse, and relational difficulties.

As most of the support services are founded on the theory of evolution, it is natural to conclude that the causes for such outcomes are due to human relational and environmental factors alone. The support provided by either state or private means aims to meet or replace some of these unmet emotional needs. Therapists often use a form of "limited parenting," offering themselves as temporary attachment figures as part of the therapeutic relationship. The problem with such attachments are the difficulties people face once therapy ends or services are withdrawn.

Now, it is true that unmet emotional needs are the root cause of many of the mental, physical, and social functioning issues we face today. However, this does not go far enough, as it tends to be one-dimensional, focusing solely on human-to-human interaction. This view does not consider that we are spiritual beings created by God in His image. The primary cause for our dysfunction is either overlooked, denied, or deliberately ignored. Religious views do not often help here either, blanketing everything under the term *sin, without fully explaining what sin actually is or means.*

Defining Sin

I am sure we are all too familiar with the caricature of the wild-haired preacher, holding the Bible in one hand as he pounds the pulpit with the other. With spittle flowing everywhere, he seeks to warn of the impending judgement and displeasure of God because of sin. The preacher presents in gory detail the graphic depiction of hellfire, where sinners will roast forever and ever. The only thing these types of messages do is to either fill the heart with fear or confirm people in their unbelief. Who wants to believe in a God that takes delight in torturing those who choose to not believe and accept Him forever and ever and ever? Not even Hitler was this unmerciful!

And all the while, the idea or concept of sin is not explained. So please bear with me as I attempt to provide a simple explanation for what really is a complicated topic. I also realise that this topic of sin is very much distasteful to most people, believers and unbelievers alike. But sin is the alternative explanation for why we humans are prone to mental, physical, and social dysfunction, not just impaired human relationships, and adverse environments alone. Sin calls us beyond the human and up to the Creator. Sin as a reason puts God firmly in the centre. But what is sin?

The plainest verse in the Holy Bible that defines sin is found in 1 John 3:4. All the various translations practically state the same thing. Sin is breaking the law. The law referred to here is often interpreted as the law God gave to Moses or the Ten Commandments. Moses was given a transcript of commands given by God for humans to adhere to, but not in the way often taught. By the time Moses received the Ten Commandments, humanity had been in a disconnected, fallen state for many years. The law served as a reminder of two main things: a) What is required from us by God; and b) our inability to obey God's requirements.

The Ten Commandments are really a magnified version of the original command given to Adam at the beginning, in the single restriction placed on them (Adam is the generic name for the first human, male and female). In choosing to disobey, Adam broke every single one of those commandments. Time or space does not permit me to break this down, but please believe that every one of those commandments was contained in that one command that was broken. Even more consequential was that now that Adam had chosen to disobey, they could no longer choose of themselves to obey. They had disconnected themselves from the source of life and power and were now facing death as the command demanded. God, in His mercy towards humankind, devised a plan in which the penalty would fall on Him, giving humanity another chance. This is why the law of Moses, or the Ten Commandments, came with the sacrificial system.

Missing The Mark.

From both the Hebrew and Greek languages, in which the Bible was originally written, sin is defined as "to miss" or "to miss the mark." Sin means to fall short of meeting a required standard. The standard required was obedience by faith to the command or Word of God. It was by faith because the first Adam had no idea what death was or had any knowledge of evil. All Adam knew at this point was good. Obedience by faith produced rightness or righteousness, alignment with the law or conditions for life to continue. All of this was held in place by connection through a relationship with God. The evidence was Adam being the reflection of His character of love, His image and likeness. The first Adam was able to independently choose and meet the required standard and through the laws of reproduction and heredity, this ability would be passed on to subsequent generations.

Instead, the reverse is now the reality. The inability to meet the required standards or conditions for life has been replicated. By choosing to doubt God's Word and disobey, Adam could not reverse the choice. He could no longer independently meet the required conditions for life to continue, demonstrated by their rightness or righteousness. By choosing to disobey, the first stage of death was instant. The connection to God in their spirit died. Humans are now disconnected from the source of life, just as a branch is cut from a tree. The branch does not show signs of death immediately, but a slow decaying process has begun. We really should not exist today and would not exist if God had not already provided the antidote. God foreknew that for a period of time, this earth would be disconnected from Him and so He placed within its creation the ability to reproduce, to keep natural life going.

Heart of the Gospel

Introducing the Real Matrix

I am sure we are all familiar with the popular *Matrix* movie series. In fact, the term "matrix" is bandied about so much today, especially among those who have been labelled conspiracy theorists. (It is funny how much of what has been first denounced as a conspiracy has actually proven to be true. But I digress). The truth is (and here I go) that we have all been born into a matrix. As humans we are dual-natured, being both physical and spiritual, but we are now, because of sin, locked solely into the physical realm.

Remember, we discussed earlier that when God first created humans, they were placed in a garden east of Eden. Eden is symbolic of the spiritual realm where God and other non-material beings reside. A consequence of disobedience was the removal or ejection of Adam from Eden. A similar theme of Man losing his first dominion crops up in so many myths, legends, and even storylines for popular movies. Truth is often mingled with fiction. By virtue of disobedience and, dare I say it, the mercy of God in postponing the full consequences of Adam's choice to not agree with the conditions for life, we, through the laws of reproduction and heredity, are born locked into the physical realm.

Being locked into the physical or material world or realm does not mean we are no longer spiritual. We are still spirit beings, but we have lost the connection to our source. All we now reproduce is the fallen human nature, unable of itself to meet the conditions for life in all its forms to continue. We are all born under the condemnation of the law that is written in our very DNA.

By choosing to disobey, Adam chose death for all of us. Romans 5:12 puts it this way, ***"Therefore, just as sin came into the world through one man, and death came through sin, and so death spread to all because all have sinned".*** As a consequence of one man's decision, we all are suffering the fallout. Why? Because each of us has inherited the inability to meet the conditions of life. We have inherited a fallen spiritual nature that is naturally self-orientated and disconnected from God. Adam chose the knowledge of Good and Evil. This is what we see conflicting our world today. Despite all our endeavours to secure a balance between these two opposing forces, we are ever further away from doing so. Good and evil, life and death were never to co-exist. They are antagonistic to each other.

This is the root cause of all our emotional and psychological issues, both individually and collectively. Instead of being *"all good,"* we are now a mixture of good and evil and this is displayed in our world. We sin because we are sinful. Sin is often defined by actions or behaviours in both the religious and secular arenas. The criminal justice system is all about punishing and correcting wrong behaviours, which can be physically seen and addressed. Religious systems are all about pointing out, condemning, and correcting wrong behaviours that are also physically seen. Very rarely are we informed that we do wrong because by nature we are wrong. Each one of us carries deep down inside a sense of not being good enough, not meeting some standard or condition. Often this is externalized into not meeting some worldly expectation, but the real cause is way beyond this. In the next chapters, we will look deeper into what we all have inherited.

Chapter 2:

What we have Inherited

Genesis 3 tells the familiar version of how humans fell by succumbing to temptation and choosing to disobey the command of God not to eat from the Tree of Knowledge. Most people today view this story as a fable that teaches a moral lesson but not an actual event. Questions have arisen concerning the validity or truthfulness of the account because it seems too simple. Everyone's destiny lies in the choice to eat or not eat the fruit of a tree. The account given in Genesis, however, is an attempt to convey a spiritual reality in a form that can be understood by our fallen nature. We are now locked into the material realm where everything is concrete and literal. By making this choice, our first human parents disconnected themselves from God spiritually and became subject to death. Technically, it should have ended right there for humans, but God, in His infinite love and mercy, had prepared a way by which humans can be restored back into divine favour, with God Himself paying the heavy price to do so.

The laws and emotional needs that are originally designed to connect us in relationship with God can no longer fulfil their original purpose and have, in fact, become a huge part of the "sin" problem. The laws and emotional needs still seek to be fulfilled, they are hardwired in us, but because we are no longer connected to God, and by the law of heredity are born disconnected from God, these needs and laws can no longer achieve their intended goals.

Furthermore, having lost the "living" connection to God in the spiritual nature, humans have been locked "spiritually" into the natural material nature or body, which has distorted the perceptions of reality and continues to do so by the laws of the mind. The emotional and psychological needs which are intrinsic to our spiritual nature, we now try to fulfil by using the material world around us, including each other. Attempting to meet our own emotional needs is often what is behind our behaviours that lead to excesses and addictions.

Before the Fall

Before the fall, in Genesis 2:25, both male and female humans were naked and without shame. There was complete openness, nothing to hide, as they had no knowledge of anything other than what God had at this point allowed. They were in full obedience, total innocence, and ignorant of any knowledge outside of what God intended them to have, which was the knowledge of good. You could say that at this point, humans, although fully formed with adult bodies, were like children in their innocence and trust. Everything they needed was freely supplied in abundance.

While in connection with God, there was complete harmony between male and female. The balance was complete. There was none of the disharmony and struggle for dominance that now takes place between males and females. In connection with God, male and female were able to be completely naked, open with each other, entirely without shame. Male Adam saw himself in the female, the female saw herself in the male (bone of my bone, flesh of my flesh). Both male and female Adam saw themselves openly before God in connection and relationship with Him. Each also stood independently, having perfect control over themselves. It is through this threefold relationship, with God, with others and with self, that humans were able to have dominion over the earth. Humans, at this point were not "self-aware" in the negative sense we are today. There was no sense of threat, of conflict, or of being alone. In this state, the new creation enjoyed true Sabbath rest!

Self-Awareness Brings New Emotions

Following the choice to disobey in Genesis 3:7, we learn that both their eyes were opened, and they saw they were naked. The opening of the eyes mentioned does not refer to literal sight. The mental perceptions of what they were observing changed. They were happily naked before without issue, but now they had a deep sense of *shame* that led them to cover up from each other. Shame is defined in psychology as the deep innate sense of the self being wrong, as opposed to guilt, which we sense from doing wrong. Directly after transgressing the divine instruction, both the male and female had a deep sense of shame that led to them covering up from each other. This was not a sexual thing, in that they realised their nakedness and sexual differences. This was a result of the now broken laws of the mind on their perceptions. The innocence and ignorance they once possessed were gone. They now had new information to process, the knowledge of shame and guilt and self-awareness now they had disconnected themselves from God.

Instead of approaching God as they heard Him walking in the garden, they hid among the trees because they were afraid. Being afraid is the same as being anxious or fearful. *Fear* is the unpleasant emotion felt when under threat or danger. The perceptions now sense fear instead of love approaching as they saw themselves as naked and could no longer be in God's presence.

This new form of "self-awareness" carried with it the knowledge of *guilt* and led to the pair hiding from God in the garden. It also led to the self-justifying attitude of the pair when questioned by God regarding what they had done. Each blamed the other and ultimately God Himself, rather than admit their wrong. Does this sound familiar to us humans today? We all have inherited this defence mechanism to protect the "self" from exposure. All humans hide to some degree to protect self.

The disobedience of the pair led to them being expelled from the Garden of Eden and prevented by their own efforts to return. Although the exclusion was to be temporary, that a way was made to return, this promise could not remove the sense of *rejection* from failing or missing the mark, which is the biblical definition of sin. Every human heart is stamped with this sense of rejection, of not being right.

Disconnection from God Changes the Heart.

There is no change in the heart of God towards humans. We are still very much beloved and wanted. Disobedience, however, has caused a permanent change in our hearts towards God by the very laws that were designed in our nature to connect us to Him. Our nature has changed, which prevents those laws operating as they should. Sin has made humans *narcissistic* and under the control of death through *rebellion* and separation. Our minds either deny or run from God, or seek to appease Him, earn His favour and ward off death through a distorted understanding of His character.

The law of heredity works against us in reproducing the sinful nature with which we are born. *Fear* is the unpleasant emotion felt when a threat to life is perceived. There is no greater threat to life than death itself, which is now in our world because of sin. God does not condemn us. It is the encoded laws within us that create the sense of inadequacy and condemnation as they are broken. The Gospel is the message of His love and plan to redeem us from this awful conundrum.

The theory of evolution attempts to account for why death is present in our world. The theory concludes that death is necessary to remove the weak, mutated, and unproductive, in order to make room for the younger, the more productive, and stronger, summed up in the famous statement, "Only the fittest can survive." Yet this explanation raises questions, as alluded to in Part One. Why do we then care for the weak and unproductive amongst us?

Why do we fight so hard for them to survive? Or mourn the loss when they die? Are these not moral duties and responsibilities?

Although we still retain the capacity to love and connect to others, our natural self-awareness interferes with our perceptions and abilities to connect. The transgressed laws continue to inform us of our inherited *rebellion, narcissism, shame, guilt, fear, and rejection*. They are an innate part of our human nature, and just like genes, they are expressed according to our biology and the environment we are nurtured in.

Chapter 3:

What we have Inherited: Rebellion

The fall of man is a theological term used to explain why this earth, originally created in harmony and connection with God, has now changed into the world of suffering and disharmony we see everywhere. We looked at the implications of the decision to disobey the one command or restriction placed upon us. All humans now, as a consequence, inherit a personality that is opposed to God and unable to obey or conform to spiritual law. As Adam chose death instead of life, all living things die that were placed under their dominion. This is cold, hard justice. Even though heavily influenced by the serpent (as told in Genesis), Adam freely chose to reject God's Word in favour of another.

The Law of Life: Self-Denial and Self-Control.

Questions have always arisen concerning the nature of God and where He came from, but these and other such questions cannot be fully answered. Huge numbers choose not to believe there is a God because no satisfactory answers can be found. They happily conclude that God is non-existent. Unbeknown to them, their choice to disbelieve actually proves the possibility of God existing. We cannot deny anything that does not exist. Whether literal or even as just an idea, in some form it is there. Those who choose not to believe also do not realise that it is because God places Himself under limits and respects our choice, that we are not zapped into non-existence for our audacity to even question whether He is real!

Our unbelief shows the level of ignorance and darkness that we humans are in. We have fallen so far from our original place and purpose that we no longer recognise who we truly are. We are so locked in this material world (THE TRUE MATRIX), that we believe and teach life came from nothing, and that we evolved from a blob to a primate into humans to sit at the top of the animal kingdom. By denying we were created in the image of God, we fail to acknowledge that we are the link species between the material and spiritual realms, and there are other beings that reign above us. Humans were given dominion of this earth only, not the vast universe in which it is contained.

The universe itself produces a legitimate argument for the existence of God. The universe cannot be quantified, it is limitless. Where do the boundaries of the universe begin or end? Scientists still have no clue despite all their attempts to measure and find out. They can only give theories and guesstimates. But the universe, as vast as it is, is somehow contained. It does not spin off into nothing. There are predictable patterns within it. The universe, in all its vastness, is constrained by laws. The universe reflects the all-powerful God who made it. A God who is beyond all limits and yet willingly restricts Himself to the boundaries of His own laws. Why? Simply because power is not defined by being without limits. That just leads to despotism and destruction. To be infinite and yet be able to contain oneself within limits is where true power resides. True power requires two things, self-denial, and self-control.

The Creator God, who is omnipotent and boundless, restrains Himself within the moral law(s) or universal covenant. All creatures, both human and non-human with higher intelligence, are required also to discipline themselves to self-denial and self-control. These principles preserve order. No kingdom can continue without some form of order or government. No kingdom can exist without laws to maintain that order. Even in our fallen state, human governments reflect this. To be law-abiding citizens, we must choose to follow or stay within the prescribed legal limits. We can choose to break the law but many of us do not. The majority of us obey out of fear of the consequences or penalties incurred if we do not, sometimes inwardly hating that we have to.

It is About Order, not Gender

The representation of God's authority was to be reflected in the created order, positions, and roles assigned by God to the male and female. God created the male Adam first. Before God formed the woman, He had already designated the male to be the ultimate responsibility and accountability for the earth. Only to the male did God directly impart the instruction regarding the Tree of Knowledge and its penalty of death. This is particularly important and will be clearer as we continue on.

It is beyond any cultural influences, or other ideas promoted, why God is represented in the male. It really has nothing to do with physical biology or gender definitions. It has everything to do with order, rank, or position. The male represents God as the originator, source, instigator, and initiator of everything. A verse in scripture puts it this way, "All things were created by Him and for Him, and He is before all things, and by Him all things consist." (Colossians1:16-17). God, in His position and authority, is represented as the ***male.*** It naturally follows that all of His creation is represented as ***female***. As stated, this is not in the context of biology or gender, but in order, rank and positioning, regardless of the biological sex. In short, **ALL** things created relate to God in the female position, whether biologically male or female. So, what is the female position?

Going back to creation, God formed a woman from the rib of Adam to be his helper. The use of a rib taken from the side indicates equality of value and purpose. However, the female being created from the male is naturally placed in the secondary position of rank and authority. God placed upon the male the responsibility and accountability to

Heart of the Gospel

sustain, protect, and love the woman. The woman in turn was to respect and submit to the divine authority placed within the male.

The position order placed upon the male and female was necessary to reflect the nature of God's government. Government or kingdom rulership originates not with humans but with God Himself. In a simple nutshell, you cannot have a kingdom without subjects or the governed. Likewise, God cannot be a ruler or king without having a creation to rule over. By virtue of being the Creator, the source of life, God has the right to set the conditions and boundaries of those whom He has brought into existence. By the same virtue, God is responsible and accountable for His creation.

Before the fall, there was no disharmony between the male and female. Both accepted their positions and were completely open to each other, being naked and without shame. In their innocence, there was no recognition of the biological differences between the male and female as a bad or immoral thing, nor the differences in gender or roles assigned. This all changed when they listened to the voice of the serpent and disobeyed. But in order to bring about the fall, there had to be a subversion of the natural order between them.

Rebellion Changes Natural Order.

Before the woman was created, God placed male Adam in the garden of Eden, which was to be his home with the purpose of working to keep the garden from becoming overrun. Any gardener can testify that keeping natural growth in check is necessary. Adam was also placed in the garden to guard and protect it from becoming corrupted by remaining obedient to the command God gave not to eat of the Tree of Knowledge. Upon male Adam was placed the responsibility, through the exercise of free will, to subdue the earth and keep out the powers of evil and death. Evil and

Heart of the Gospel

death exist as a natural byproduct of free will. God is love, and love does not compel or force obedience. It has to be freely given. God gave to man all that is good for life. By allowing choice, the alternatives of evil and death, become possible, but only Man's choice can bring them into existence.

The serpent, or snake, is the animal used to enter the garden with the assumed purpose of bringing rebellion to the newly created earth. The serpent bypassed the male and engaged in a conversation about the Tree of Knowledge with the woman. Instead of consulting with the male, the woman continued to dialogue with the serpent, and the rest we know is history. Humans were given dominion over the earth, including all creatures, including the serpent.

But here we find the serpent discussing the Tree of Knowledge with the woman, who, in turn, attempts to exert her authority by adding to the command that God gave, stating they were not to even touch the fruit as they would die. Instead of recognizing the need to get the male input on this discussion, the woman usurped her position and fell right into the deception and ended up eating the fruit. When the woman eats the fruit, nothing happens. It is not until the male also eats the forbidden fruit that both their eyes are opened, and they see their nakedness in a shameful way. Why the male made the choice to listen to the woman and follow her in eating from the forbidden tree is not clearly stated. What is obvious is the fact that male Adam was ***not deceived***. This was a deliberate choice to go against the command given to him by God.

Reversed Order Fixed

There has been a lot of theological content I have purposely missed out because I want to focus on the effects we now suffer from the fall and not the how and why. I will, however, be closing this section of the book with the chapter "A Peep Behind the Veil", which does go into the context.

Heart of the Gospel

You can pause and read that chapter now and come back if it will help.

Our first parents' decisions have resulted in us being born with an aversion to submission and a genuinely disordered nature. The serpent or snake was from the lower animal kingdom and as such should not have been given the scope it took. The serpent's questions appeared to rouse the appetite and desires; the animal urges inherent in the physical body. The woman, sensing or experiencing the stimulation, was led to make the decision to eat based on ***emotions.*** In the excitement this might have produced, the woman went to the male and encouraged him to eat. At this point, the male had the ***rational*** choice. He knew eating the fruit was wrong. He knew death (whatever that was) would be the result, but the woman had not changed. He knew what God *had* told him, but he could *hear* what the woman was saying. He chose to listen to her and ate the fruit too.

The first thing that occurred afterwards was a change in their perceptions. They saw themselves and their surroundings differently. They noticed they were naked, and it was not a good thing. Something had been drastically altered. The changes happened only after the male ate. Male Adam had a conflicting choice to make. Choosing to obey the command at this point would mean denying the woman, which would mean denying himself. Remember, the woman was bone of his bone and flesh of his flesh. In choosing to listen to the woman, he chose to listen to a part of himself. Instead of keeping the command God gave him, male Adam completed the subversion of the divine order by placing his reasoning above God. Once the decision had been made to disregard the command of God in place of his own reasoning, it could not be reversed.

This decision, however, was not limited to just disregarding the one restriction or command given. This decision affected all laws or commands instituted by God to govern and sustain life on earth. In choosing himself, man lost the ability to fully control his own physical drives and emotions. He lost the ability to independently obey all laws, internal and external, without being induced by some fearful consequence. If we are left to ourselves to do our own thing without some system of authority to compel us, we would self-destruct. And if we should take a brutally honest look at our world today, we can see it happening as old moral and institutional guidelines are being demolished under the pretext of freedom and equality for all.

Why Parenting is a Tough Job.

Rebellion is the germinating seed for the disobedience found, sadly, within every human being since the fall. We all are inclined towards doing our own thing, wanting to go our own way. We see this clearly in the natural disposition of our children. Parenting has much to do with subduing the innate inclination to defy authority and want our own way. Rebellion is within the heart of us all. This may seem an offensive statement to make, but unless we are aware of the spiritual realm around us, we cannot see how the modern society we live in is built on the principles of rebellion. We cannot see that we are participating in a rebellion against the government and authority of God.

We cannot see that the current crisis we are having globally with mental health disorders has some roots in the subversion of the divinely ordained order between males and females. We are led to look at things from a solely biological and gender-based basis without realising that any deviation is the continued outworking of rebellion against God. We cannot see how often we put *emotional* reasoning above what is *rational,* to our detriment. We cannot see how our lives have been narrowed down to fulfilling perverted physical drives and self-preservation.

Evolution effectively eradicates or undermines the existence of God by replacing God with science. Religion perverts the true character and nature of God by making Him appear as a Being that needs to be appeased to extract any blessings, who delights in the suffering of humans. Or impotent, leaving humans to get on with it, as taught by "Deists" whose theories have majorly influenced our modern world. But where we really get our opinions about God are from how we have been parented and often characterise Him as being the same. So many have rejected God as being a Father by this same analogy. So many of us struggle with the concept of trusting a loving God that we cannot physically see, because we have been so traumatised and unloved by the parents we could.

Reproducing Rebellion

The natural inclination of wanting to have or go our own way, to despise authority and rules, unless they serve the purpose of getting our own needs met, has been hardwired into us and replicated through the laws of heredity and reproduction. We may appear dutiful and compliant as we go about our daily lives, as long as the status quo is supplying what we need. Should the status quo change, restrict or stop supplying our needs then our rebellious nature is revealed. We go on strike, demonstrate, engage in acts of civil disobedience, and even go to war.

Of course, this is seen as lawfully exercising our rights, demonstrating against unfairness, and protecting the weak from the strong. We conclude that it is necessary at times to go against a system of management or government that is unjust, for the good of the majority. History is full of accounts where leaders have been ousted from power by the refusal of people to co-operate or continue to follow their leadership. The truth is we have made rebellion legally acceptable in preserving another aspect of our fallen human nature which is narcissism, self-love, and self-preservation.

Chapter 4:

What we have Inherited: Narcissism

The topic of narcissism has never been as popular as it is today. Everywhere on social media, experts, whether professionally trained or not, attempt to define the symptoms or traits that make up the narcissistic personality. Everyone is on the lookout to identify a narcissist without realising that they see one every time they look in the mirror. Narcissism is inherent in every one of us as part of our fallen human nature, but it does, as with all psychological and personality issues, trend along a continuum. Most of us fall into the "healthy narcissist" category, which psychologists classify as being normal. After all, you do have to have some regard for yourself and your own needs. The unfortunate ones who are diagnosed as having narcissistic personality disorder (professionally or not) take self-regard to an extreme level where everything is all about them.

We are all narcissistic when we realise that it is primarily self-centeredness. Psychiatry denies the existence of God and is itself a form of legal rebellion. The Diagnostic and Statistical Manual of Mental Disorders 5 (DSM-5) or the International Classification of Diseases 10 (ICD-10) are used by psychiatrists and mental health professionals worldwide to diagnose and treat mental health disorders. They attempt to make mental health disorders and behaviours a dysfunction that can be treated by medication or therapy alone. The truth is such efforts only provide a temporary resolution, with continual relapses leading to lifelong dependence on such services.

By denying the existence of God, they have removed the knowledge of our spiritual nature, the root cause of the dysfunctional behaviours categorised in the manual, aside from an organic dysfunction of the brain itself. By denying the existence of God, they remove the only true source of healing for the unmet emotional and psychological needs that have caused the disorders to be there in the first place.

Not Enough Figleaves.

Narcissism is a personality disorder that we all have and as mentioned before, can be measured along a continuum. Our personalities are truly disordered when we realise that we were created to reflect the image and likeness (personality) of God. Those who sadly meet the diagnostic criteria are the individuals whose parents or early caregivers did not provide adequate "figleaf" covering to hide the narcissism, rebellion, shame, guilt, rejection, and fear we have inherited. It is the same for all diagnosed or listed personality disorders. Not enough figleaves!

According to the Cambridge English Dictionary, the term "figleaf" is defined as "something that hides something else, especially something that is dishonest or embarrassing". The Free Dictionary goes further by stating that the figleaf is the innocuous (innocent) appearance used to cover up an act or object that is embarrassing or distasteful, and directly references the Garden of Eden and the fall of Man.

Parenting is the continual attempt to meet all the emotional, social, cognitive, and physical development needs of the growing child while subduing and retraining the natural narcissistic tendencies, in order for the child to become someone who can be successful and confident in social engagement and relationships. We encourage our children to share, to think of others, and to be part of a team. Parenting attempts to restrain the natural impulses to want our own way and do things how we think best; to better hide our inborn orientation to be self-absorbed and self-preserving so we can become positive members of society; to be able to form attachments to other people outside our immediate family circle and fit in. The more able we are to form attachments with others, the more successful we are likely to be in life. When you take a look over the grand scheme of things, life is mostly about relationships, whether positive or negative.

We are Born Egocentric.

Of all the creatures born, the human infant is the most helpless and dependent for the longest time. This is due to the immaturity of our brains and nervous system. The neocortex layer of our brains at birth is scantily formed with the necessary neural pathways and connections required. These connections are influenced by the environment we are born into. Unlike other mammals, human infants cannot start walking within a few days or weeks. A calf can soon find its mum and suckle when hungry or run with the herd when in danger. A human infant can do neither of these things for a while. As a consequence, from birth (or even before), the human threat response is switched on. It needs to be, simply because we are born into a world where death is very much present.

An infant would die in a matter of days if not taken care of by the adults in its environment. A baby or young child has no way of meeting its own needs. The ability to form strong attachments is not a luxury or out of love. At this stage of our development, it is all about survival. No matter how harsh or difficult the family unit we have been born into, each of us will adapt in numerous ways to survive, to have our emotional and psychological needs met. The world has to revolve around us. Self has to be the centre of attention. Our lives depend on never being forgotten. So human babies are constantly sending out signals to those around them. They need to be kept close, attended to, and fussed over.

An infant at this stage of development is unable to understand anything other than what is necessary to soothe

the threat response. All of this is done instinctively. If a little one feels the pangs of hunger, they would normally signal through crying that they need to be fed. This infant does not compute or care that the adults may not have slept for five nights, are in pain, or are unable to cope. The baby needs what it needs, and it needs it now. Life depends on this. Fortunately, for most of us, the caregiving adults provide good enough care to meet our emotional and physical needs. Through repetition and consistency, the threat response is soothed and as the child matures, confidence is gained that its needs will always be met. The child does not have to signal so hard to be acknowledged.

As time goes on, the child quickly learns how to keep in the good graces of the family to retain the necessary meeting of emotional, physical, and psychological needs. We learn very quickly how to suppress or hide the parts of us that are not considered healthy for social relationships, and having a steady enough supply enables us to be less focused on ourselves. We can explore the world around us, understand the needs of others, and make strong connections. This is known broadly as having a secure attachment pattern. In child development circles, this attachment pattern is the desired outcome parents should aim for as it gives us as children the best start in life to succeed.

Good Attachment Is Never Enough.

But even in the best of endeavours to provide a secure attachment pattern, our efforts would never be enough to supply the level of need. Even if we have the best health, financial, and educational advantages, and complete stability, (which some do), it would still not be enough. The emotional and psychological needs are greater than what any human can supply. They are hardwired within us to attach to God in relationship first and with others after. Despite our best efforts in parenting, there will always be a gap. Psychologists have learned this very well and encourage "good enough" parenting as being the benchmark to reach. This is why even with a good secure attachment pattern, we can still struggle with inadequacy and shame. Of not being good enough. We then blame ourselves and feel incredible guilt for having these thoughts and feelings. Or we suppress them and project our inadequacies onto others or attempt to soothe ourselves by comparing and contrasting against those who have not been as fortunate.

As stated before, whatever environment we are born into, our primary need for survival is to attach to the adult caregivers around us. A child will make huge adaptations to ensure they stay in some form of relationship. A child or young person is unable to calculate all the risks involved. They only know instinctively or intuitively that they need this person. Even in horrific cases of mistreatment, a child still wants to stay with the abuser while at the same time wanting to avoid them leading to a disorganised attachment pattern. One minute they are clingy, then the next pushing away. The threat underpinning this type of attachment is the fear of complete abandonment. To a helpless and dependent child or young person, abandonment is akin to death. Whatever the cost to prevent desertion, we will agree to it. The hefty price of our developing personality is what we pay.

For myriads of reasons, many of us have been unable to achieve or experience a secure enough attachment pattern within our family unit. For many, parenting has been complicated by external factors as well as internal. The world or society that we now live in is not conducive to building strong relationships with our children, who spend many hours separated from us while we work and toil to provide for their physical needs. The emotional and psychological often take a back seat. Many of us are victims of insecure and traumatic attachment during childhood and are still emotionally shut down in protective mode when we have children. None of us are as virtuous as we like to believe. Every one of us who has become parents has attempted in some way to get our unmet emotional needs supplied by our children.

This is often done imperceptibly and unintentionally under the guise of wanting the best for our children. Secretly we feed off their success and get some gratification when they are acknowledged for doing well. There are those parents who see themselves in a superior position to their children when they fail. We often hide our own desire for attention, acceptance, affirmation, and affection, by pouring our all into our children so we can get it second-hand through their achievements. Some parents even reverse the role of parenting and expect their children to supply their needs and take care of them.

Narcissism is our Self-Centred World.

I hope you are beginning to recognise that we are all in some way narcissistic. We cannot help being this way, it is now very much a part of our survival, part of the drive for self-preservation. The difference is how we have learned through our childhood experiences to mask or suppress the innate urge toward self. How confident we have learned to trust other people to be there for us, to supply our emotional needs. Being in relation with others helps to reduce the intense self-awareness that is a reminder of our inherited sin. The greater the disconnection from God, from others, and our inner selves, the more urgent the efforts to signal to others to get our needs met, even in negative ways.

The emotional needs that were designed to be met primarily by God Himself first, and then shared with others, are now a cause of human dysfunction. Unable to receive directly from God because of the separation caused by sin, we attempt to get our emotional needs fulfilled by other humans, leading to exploitation and oppression.

The continual exploitation and oppression of humans across the ages have formed the modern world we know today. To be honest, nothing has changed regarding the fundamental structures of society across the many centuries of civilisation. There has always existed a division between the few who have and the many who have not. Every political movement has attempted to provide a more equal society. Capitalism, communism, fascism, socialism, and every other "ism" has attempted to attain a fairer share for everyone. Each has, and will, continue to miserably fail.

The emotional need for acceptance, attention, affirmation, affection, protection, guidance, discipline, and comfort instinctively causes us to selfishly seek our own interests. The drive to dominate and be in control directs the setting up of standards that dictate how these emotional needs are to be secured apart from a relationship with God. These manmade standards or laws vainly attempt to provide a covering for our inherited narcissism.

Chapter 5:

What we have Inherited: Shame and Guilt

We all at some point in our lives experience episodes of low self-esteem or depression as a natural reaction to the stresses of life. Fortunately, for the majority of us, depression is short-lived, and we can bounce back and continue engaging in life. For others, depression is the primary position for them. Some continue to engage with living but not to their full potential. Others do not even attempt to try anymore and give in to the deep dark feelings. Wherever there is depression, you will find at least one of these negative emotional/psychological states in activation.

Our tendency to feel shame and guilt is not entirely a product of early childhood or negative life events, as psychologists inform us. These states, along with fear, rebellion, narcissism, and rejection, are inborn mental states we have inherited as part of our natural fallen nature. The environment that we have been nurtured in or currently live in does play a considerable role in how these states are expressed and how badly they affect our day-to-day functioning. If we are honest with ourselves, we would admit to struggling internally against shame or guilt, in some form. We struggle because they involve the moral qualities of being right or wrong.

Shame.

Shame and guilt are often mistaken as being the same thing, but they are not. We can feel ashamed of our actions, especially if they have hurt others, but shame is not about what we have done. Shame is about who we are. Guilt is about what we do. Here is a clinical definition of shame. "A distressing emotion involving a strong sense of having transgressed against a social or moral code; it is a feeling that a person is, at their core, bad or wrong. A pervasive, negative emotional state, usually originating in childhood, marked by chronic self-reproach and a sense of personal failure." (The American Heritage Medical Dictionary, 2007).

Shame is the inner emotional state produced by a perceived failure to meet the required standard for acceptance. It is understood that from as early as six months, an infant can experience shameful feelings, which are often seen as they drop their heads and avert their eyes . Shame becomes more prominent as we develop more self-awareness. Between the ages of six and twelve months, brain development continues at a rapid pace. During this period, infants become aware that they are a separate entity, triggering the development phase known as separation anxiety. A baby usually becomes clingy and upset if left with people they do not know. Birth brings about the first huge separation shock on a physical level as the baby leaves the womb. Self-awareness brings the second separation shock on the spiritual level and with it a subtle awareness, on a primitive level, of our fallen state.

As we grow older, our attachment needs start to change their focus. Attachment is not only motivated by having our physical needs supplied. We now seek to be connected emotionally, to be constantly reassured that we are okay, because something deep down is telling us we are not. Toddlers especially seek frequent reassurance that they are loved and doing well. They need positive feedback to enable them to develop a more confident reflection of who they are. You see, the negative is already in situ. We are born condemned. The truth is, we do not have to be told we are wrong. We have this knowledge in us already. A negative environment repeatedly confirms what we intuitively know. A negative environment makes it harder to overcome the sense of shame leading to the development of anxiety and depression from an early age. It is the transgressed laws that are embedded and stimulated within that are the deeper reason we experience shame.

Guilt.

Having understood the definition of shame as an internal sense of being wrong, guilt is the internal sense of doing wrong. Psychologists believe guilt cannot fully be experienced before three years of age. The neocortex, in particular the frontal lobes, needs to be connected and functioning to be able to appreciate the differences between right and wrong. Most of the understanding comes from a non-verbal, implicit sense rather than a verbal or cognitive sense. As young children, we can sense we are doing something wrong without actually knowing what the wrong is. We read the non-verbal or emotional clues from our environment and respond accordingly. The ability to reason from cause to effect, to understand logically why a behaviour or action is wrong comes a lot later.

Between the ages of zero to seven years, we are very egocentric in our worldview. The world revolves around us. If the adults around us are happy, we believe it is because of us. If the adults around us are unhappy, we believe we have made them unhappy. Our need to attach and remain in connection is still directed by our need to survive. Even if it means subconsciously assimilating the guilt of others, taking the responsibility and blame by applying it to ourselves so they will not be upset or rejected, we will do it. There are many adults today struggling with a whole load of guilt that is not a consequence of what they have personally done. Without awareness, they have decided long ago that if they do not take responsibility, something worse will happen. As a therapist, I see this reasoning a lot when working with people who have obsessive-compulsive disorder, or OCD, an anxiety disorder very much driven by feelings of guilt and responsibility.

Heart of the Gospel

According to the prominent psychoanalyst Erik Erikson's stages of psychosocial development, there are specified life stages or conflicts we must successfully navigate or pass through in developing a healthy personality. Between the ages of three and five, we enter the ***"initiative vs guilt"*** stage where we want to explore and attempt new things and be independent. During this phase, we try to do things ourselves and realise that we cannot. Erikson proposes that children who are positively supported are better able to manage failure and not give up. They can grow in confidence and be open to mastering new skills and achievements.

During this stage, we start questioning whether we are a good or bad person based on performance. Our thinking is very black and white, and we believe our value is based more on what we can do than on who we are. But why do we even go through this stage in the first place? As we grow older, we become more self-aware. This self-awareness exposes us to the negative emotional and psychological states we have inherited from being a fallen human. I say they are negative in the context of our original creation by God. We experience them because we are born disconnected in our inner spirit from Him. Having strong attachments externally to our caregivers helps to subdue the intensity of the effects these negative states can produce, but it cannot eradicate them completely. Those of us who have not received the benefits of a positive attachment will be exposed to this negative state of guilt a lot earlier, without the support to lessen the intensity. We are less prepared to manage the voice of the inner critic.

The Inner Critic

I am sure we all have experienced a negative voice inside our heads telling us that we have not done something right, or that we are incompetent. Welcome to the voice of the inner critic. Psychologists believe this internal talk develops during childhood as we expand our assessment of ourselves by internalising the cues gathered initially from our immediate caregivers. As we become more exposed and incorporated into the wider social platforms of school, work, and life, we learn new standards which influence our inner perceptions of self. According to Sigmund Freud's model of the human personality, the inner critic or voice is part of the superego, the part of ourselves that contains the moral codes, standards, and rules which ought to govern our behaviours, along with the sense of how worthy or acceptable we are by doing so.

If our emotional or attachment needs have not been adequately met, giving us the assurance of being worthy, acceptable, and loved, the more disconnected we will feel from others and ourselves. In our early years, this sense of disconnection was a huge threat to our survival. Psychologists believe that the voice of the inner critic develops to spur us into actions that minimize being rejected and ensure we can somehow meet the conditions required, even if this means suppressing or denying our needs. The inner critic's task is to keep the urges for our emotional needs to be met in check while prompting us to perform and meet the standards that will aid the securing of our emotional needs. This can be quite a difficult and conflicting position to find ourselves in as children. The poorer the attachment quality to our caregivers, the greater the detachment. The greater the detachment, the louder the inner critic will sound the alarm to either put us in overdrive to meet the standards or paralysis of action by informing us we cannot meet them.

The inner voice inside our heads that critiques our actions or sense of self, who demands higher expectations be reached, or punishes us for feeling or expressing an emotional need, is part of our fallen nature. After male Adam ate the fruit from the forbidden tree, they became ashamed of their nakedness. The innocence of conscience they once possessed was now swallowed up by guilt. They attempted to cover or hide their guilt and shame by making figleaf garments.

Later, when they heard God coming into the garden, they hid among the trees from His presence. In response to God calling them, male Adam responded, telling God they were hiding from Him because they were naked. The question God asks Adam is pertinent to understanding the inner critic. The question asked was, "Who told you that you were naked?" It was the voice of the inner critic that informed Adam they were no longer right because they had missed the mark and transgressed the law. Along with our inherited fallen nature comes the voice of the inner critic reminding us that we also miss the mark.

The Need to Justify Self

Being born into an inherited state of guilt naturally leaves us wanting to make ourselves right. Unbelievably, we spend most of our childhood and early years of life trying to make others love and accept us. Our survival depends on our ability to attach and connect with others to take care of us. So, any negative messages about who we are end up being deflected. Otherwise, we would completely stop signalling for our needs to be met, which could lead to death. Children, without thinking, often resort to misbehaving as a way of getting adult attention. The biological drive for self-preservation takes over. We learn very quickly to deny or override negative messages by justifying ourselves. We do this by over-inflating our sense of worth, to make our presence known. Conversely, we can collapse our sense of worth by making our presence smaller, to not be excluded. Another method is by making ourselves helpful to others, giving us the appearance of being empathetic and kind.

The latter may seem surprising. Isn't being helpful, kind, and compassionate how we should be as humans? Of course, we should endeavour to be kind and compassionate. These are qualities of our Creator God, who made us in His image and likeness. The question arises when we look deeper into what is motivating our kindness. The previous chapter discussed our inherent tendency towards narcissism. We are naturally self-orientated. It is part of our survival mechanism. Most of us are kind and caring, to stop ourselves from being selfish or being viewed as selfish by others. We have been socialised by our early years of training to hide our natural self-centeredness by justifying or denying what we really are. How many times have we given things or done things we really did not want to give or do, in order to prevent ourselves from looking bad? Or to gain the approval of others?

The need to somehow expiate this inward sense of guilt has been the instigator behind many religious and philosophical movements. External standards in our societies have become substitute guidelines used to measure how right we are. If we meet the standards, then we are okay. If we do not, then we reject the standard in favour of something else that will try to make us right. When we lose the inability to resist guilt and shame, the sense of being and doing wrong, we can no longer fight the condemning voice of the inner critic. We start agreeing with what the inner critic tells us. We imagine that other people can also see what the inner critic sees, and hide away. The earlier this happens during our formative years, the more likely we will develop a diagnosable personality disorder. Being able to justify self also protects us from fully experiencing the torments of fear and rejection.

Chapter 6:

What we have Inherited: Rejection and Fear.

Fear is identified within psychology as a primal emotional reaction to the presence of a threat or danger to life. The ability to quickly detect a potentially life-threatening situation and respond in a manner to preserve life is to our greatest advantage. Unlike other creatures, humans do not have any outward defence mechanisms such as horns or scales. We do not have poisonous sacs or barbs to stun. We are not able to run fast or for long. As infants, we are the most helpless for the longest, making us during our formative years very vulnerable to the threats that are constant in our environment.

The modern world that we now occupy is completely different from the world our ancestors lived in less than a hundred years ago. We have more appliances and gadgets to make our lives easier. Travel and transportation allow a wide variety of foods to be available all year round. We no longer have to gather or preserve to ensure we do not starve. We can predict future weather patterns more accurately, better explain the natural world, and manipulate physical laws to our advantage. With all these advances at our disposal today, shouldn't we be the most relaxed and stress-free generation? But we are not. We are dying today from more stress-related illnesses such as heart, respiratory, and circulatory problems, cancers, suicides, and personal accidents than previous generations before us.

Why We Experience Fear

According to evolutionists, which most scientists and psychologists are, the ability to experience fear is a necessity for our survival. Human evolution depended on those who, by heeding the natural fear instinct, were better able to preserve themselves and pass on their genes to subsequent generations. Being able to quickly discern potential threats was certainly a survival skill needed when humans were living in tribal groups as hunter-gatherers. It certainly made the difference between existence and extinction then, but how do we account for the fear that we still experience in our modern world? Historical data shows that as we progressed from tribal, nomadic living to our current urbanization where the majority of us live in or near a city, we have become less able to manage our threat-based emotions of fear and anxiety.

Our tribal ancestors lived simpler lives more in sync with natural rhythms. The types of threats they faced were acute, real life or death situations that were dealt with one way or another fairly quickly. The dangers tended to be more physical in type, making it possible to use up the adrenalin released by our innate threat response in either fighting or fleeing. Today, our threats tend to be more psychological with little means of physical escape. We also prefer to call this stress or anxiety rather than fear, saving the use of the term fear for the actual threat to life itself or an imagined threat such as in phobias. The fact is that both ourselves and our ancestors are still contending with the greatest threat we can face: death.

We fear because we live in a world where death is present. Evolution does not attempt to explain why death exists. The theory only concludes that death is a necessity to get rid of those with weak or corrupted genes, ensuring that only the fittest and most adaptable can survive. The Bible, however, presents a different view of why death is in our world. Death came as a result of transgressing the command or law of life, by failing to meet the standard required. Our first parents first felt fear after they disobeyed and attempted to hide from God. And since we, by default, have inherited this fallen nature, we are also unable ourselves to meet the required standard, obedience by faith. We sin because we are born sinful, disconnected from God, and under the condemnation of the law, we are appointed to die.

Fear is a Reminder.

There are three main types of threatening situations we face that cause us to experience fear. These categories are A) literal threats to life, B) psychological threats impacting our capacity to cope or manage circumstances and C) social threats which undermine our ability to connect with and be accepted by others. Interestingly, these threatening situations are linked to the purposes God created humans to accomplish. God created mankind in His image and likeness to A) exercise faith in obedience and life, B) to have dominion and control over the earth and C) to have relationships with God first and then with other humans.

Most of our diagnosable anxiety disorders fall under one of these three areas. We worry (sometimes excessively) about potential future losses or catastrophes. Deep down, we are subconsciously aware that life could end in a moment, at any time. We manage to calculate most of the risks and have relative predictability, but there will always be elements of uncertainty we cannot control. Having good connections with others and enough resources to buffer us from feeling the wants that warn us of how fragile our lives are, makes us feel more secure. Advances in medicine keep death from striking too soon, but inevitably it will come for each of us. Healthy lifestyles and cosmetic procedures can push back the ageing process but not forever. We have lost eternity, yet it remains as a faint print on our souls. Freddie Mercury once sang, "Who Wants to Live Forever", perhaps to mask the bigger question, who wants to die?

From ancient times, we have, as a race, been absorbed with warding off the grim reaper and his forerunners of loss and separation. Various rituals and relics have been universally developed to protect us from sudden disasters or to guarantee harvests and good fortune. Aspects of these rituals have become embedded in formal modes of worship and adapted to fit in with the changing times. We have earnestly sought to have control over the ever-altering world we find ourselves living in, whether on a personal, local, or global level. Even our governments are forming alliances, combining resources to combat the danger of climate change and other issues that threaten our stability.

Our Overactive Threat Response

Both psychologists and medics alike agree that we are not designed (or evolved) to deal with chronic stress and fear. Our innate threat response has been kicked into overdrive, wreaking havoc on our physical and mental health. From the turn of the last century, advances in medicine were within the biological sphere, tackling the diseases caused by viruses and bacteria. Today, the diseases we face are more lifestyle-based in origin, brought on from being burdened by chronic stress and unnatural work patterns in trying to maintain a roof over our heads, put food on the table, and provide for our families.

Being constantly in overdrive, we have turned to substances and food in an attempt to soothe the anxiety and restlessness we feel. Various forms of entertainment have been devised to distract our minds, to give a sense of being okay that does not last when the entertainment ends. We face uncertainty about how long what we have will last. Some of us have a more pragmatic view and accept that there are things in life we cannot control, that are out of our hands. But most of us try to control our situations and improve our lot, to give us a better chance of security and social acceptance.

The fear of being socially ostracized is a huge one, with deep implications for our well-being. From our earliest years, our threat response has been actively scanning for any signs of rejection, firstly within our primary family unit, and then the wider social circle. Being connected to other people is a necessity for us to reduce the sense of threat (fear) we constantly face each day. From time to time, we may wonder about how others perceive us. Sadly, for some of us, it is a constant worry. The fear of being rejected becomes overwhelming to the point that it makes connecting to others almost impossible. How many marriages or relationships are happening where neither party truly knows the other person because they are afraid to open up in case they are dismissed or invalidated?

Our sense of safety, our ability to control our situations, plan our futures and accomplish them are compromised by our innate sense of fear. We have no certainty that anything will last. One day we all must face death, leaving behind the people we love, and the successes we have achieved. Nothing can be taken with us except the fear of what will happen next. No one has genuinely come back from the dead to tell us for sure what is on the other side. On this side, we continue to battle with fear and with rejection.

A Peep behind the Veil

The Spiritual War Around Us

"And the great dragon was cast out, that old serpent called the Devil and Satan which deceiveth the whole world." Revelation 12:9.

Behind this visible, material world there is a spiritual dimension. This may sound absurd or mystical, as evolution and humanism have convinced us that this world consists only of what we can experience with our physical senses. Yet we are also subtly aware that this physical world is not all there is. Many of us are drawn to religion to help us connect to this other side. Others seek paranormal encounters or science fiction to satisfy a curiosity to understand what is out there. Countless fictional stories and movies have been made incorporating beings or events that are not from this world. I am thinking of the classics *Alice in Wonderland* by Lewis Carroll or *The Lion, The Witch and The Wardrobe* by C.S Lewis as examples, or even the famous *Lord of the Rings* series or *Star Wars*... The list could go on and on. Even though they were written by different authors at different times, they all seem to contain the same themes – humans uniting with or in opposition against beings from different realms or dimensions, battling for supremacy, always involving good and evil or light and darkness.

To be honest, this theme is everywhere in our world. Even in politics and governments, we find the ***evil*** dictator whose regime must be crushed for the good and liberty of us all. Humanity tries valiantly to tackle the threats lurking everywhere in our world without fully understanding that the issues threatening our survival originate from the spiritual dimension. Anciently, this was well understood. Many of the practices that today are incorporated into religious rites and ceremonies are performances to ward off evil curses or inspire blessings from the gods.

The Symbol of the Serpent

Symbols of these extraterrestrial beings are around us every day, even incorporated into daily life such as the names of the days of the week or logos on products we buy. We are constantly exposed to the spiritual dimension but remain ignorant because there is such a distance between the sources of these symbols or logos and where we are now in time. And this ignorance has been strategically planned. Take, for instance, the universal symbol for medicine, a serpent entwined on a pole known as the Rod of Asclepius, the Greek god of healing.

Heart of the Gospel

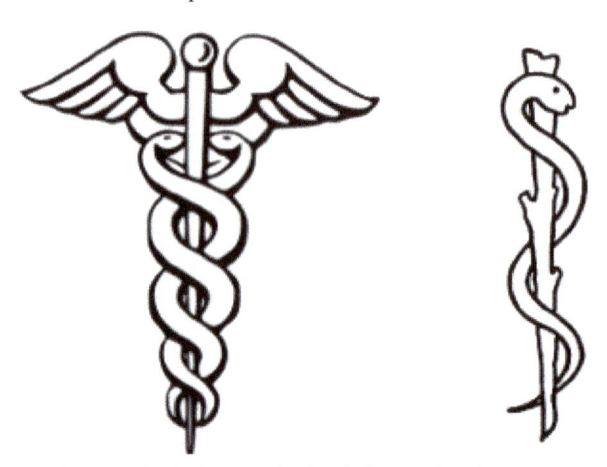

This Photo by Unknown Author is licensed under CC BY-SA

This symbol is recognised everywhere a medical facility has been established. Few of us know that this symbol of medicine is a representation of a spiritual being, a god who, according to Greek mythology, gave humans the knowledge of healing and was worshipped as the benefactor of mankind.

The Bible, however, paints a completely different picture of this spiritual being that is represented by the serpent symbol. Far from being the benefactor of humans, this spiritual being is exposed as being the instigator of the fall of man. Genesis 3 relates the sad event of how Adam (male and female) disobeyed God, fell under the penalty of death and lost their dominion over the earth. Rulership over the earth was possible only through a spiritual connection to God and this connection was lost when Adam sinned. Humanity is now locked into the material world (matrix) by the laws of heredity. The serpent was the means of occasioning the fall of man by presenting an alternative view to the express command God had given to male Adam, not to eat the fruit of the Tree of Knowledge.

Another voice is being heard speaking to Adam, but whose voice is this? The serpent itself was a beast of the field created along with the land animals on day six of the creation week. In the first verse of the chapter, the serpent is introduced as being a cunning or intelligent creature, more than any other animal formed apart from man. The serpent, however, was not created with the gift of speech. The serpent was being used as a living prop or puppet, the same way a ventriloquist does, by another spiritual being who was seeking to gain control of the earth. A detour to another book in the Bible may help to explain.

This spiritual being is mentioned within a lamentation poem God instructed the Jewish prophet Ezekiel to write. This song can be found in Ezekiel:28. Space does not permit a full rendering of the passage here, but I do urge you to read the chapter, as you will discern that these verses do not refer to a human being. Ezekiel writes of a majestic individual who once held the highest position in heaven as the anointed cherub. This being stood in the immediate presence of God and was the most beautiful, most intelligent, and musically gifted creation. Note the word "creation."

Despite the high honours and position granted to this anointed cherub, they are created. Only God is self-existing, the source of all life. Ezekiel further shares how this majestic being lost favour with God by sinning and was cast down from its high position and out of the presence of God. Verse 11 of the chapter makes certain to inform us that this being was also present in the Garden of Eden.

Hiding In Plain Sight

In another book of the Bible, this time written by the prophet Isaiah, further information on this spiritual being is supplied. God instructs the prophet Isaiah to take up a proverb, this time against the king of Babylon in ?14: 4-20This time, the name of this spiritual being and the reason for their demise is supplied. The name Lucifer, meaning "morning star" (taken from a Latin root word defined as "to shine") is revealed. What was the sin committed? Lucifer wanted to be God. To take God's place and be worshipped. In short, self-exaltation. Lucifer, this majestic, created being set himself against the Most High God, the creator and source of all life. Despite being given a throne indicating dominion and gifted with the best of everything, beauty, intelligence, musical ability etc., it was not enough. Lucifer wanted to be God. Now if this is starting to sound like a movie script or some plot in a fiction story, ask yourself the serious question, where do these ideas really come from?

If you have been able to read for yourself these verses in the Bible, both Ezekiel and Isaiah discuss this spiritual being in connection with earthly kings and the territories Babylon and Tyre. Both Babylon and Tyre are known to be historic nations of wealth and power. Babylon (now Iraq) at one time dominated the then-known world and is known as the first of the ancient nations to rule over most of the earth, with Persia, Greece, and finally Rome coming after. Tyre (now part of Lebanon) was anciently known as the place where merchants controlled trade by sea. The Babylonians were known for their knowledge and understanding of the sciences, mathematics, astronomy, law, and economics. Babylon was also the religious centre for sun worship, the sun being the symbol and identity of the chief male god Shamash, and other lesser gods.

The morning star has long been identified with the planet Venus, the brightest of the planets, usually sighted in the morning. Venus was worshipped in Babylon under the name Ishtar (where we get Easter from) or Nana and is familiarly known as the *"queen of heaven."* Both male and female deities represented Lucifer, who attempts to be androgynous, both male and female. Throughout all the nations, to this day, there are representations of the male/female god that are revered. Different names according to the language of the people, but the same god or goddess worshipped. A modern version of this androgynous god is found in the image of Baphomet, seen or referenced frequently within the movie and music industry. I hope you are beginning to see the bigger picture.

Behind our nations and governments stands a spiritual entity or entities that influence humans in their decisions and actions. Carl Jung was an instrumental figure in the formation of psychoanalysis, a form of therapy used today to understand and treat mental disorders. He understood there were "unconscious forces" that were motivating human behaviour. Jung labelled these unconscious forces Archetypes, which work in the collective unconsciousness of humans and give us commonality. The collective unconscious is defined as the knowledge that humans genetically transmit and have innately, separate from the knowledge learnt through experience (there goes that law of heredity again!). The important thing to realise is that Jung and other scientists studying the human psyche or mind have admitted there are external unseen forces exerting their influence on human behaviour.

The types and Archetypes that Jung recognised and attempted to categorise and incorporate into the human personality, are what the Bible identifies as the fallen spiritual beings that first rebelled against the government of God and found entrance to continue their rebellion here on earth.

Heart of the Gospel

Two Kingdoms Now on Earth

The serpent that spoke in the Garden of Eden was simply the tool Lucifer used to insinuate doubt concerning God, implying that He was unfairly withholding knowledge. More insidiously, Lucifer encouraged Adam to doubt the truthfulness of God's Word. By gaining the knowledge of good and evil, they would also become gods and not die as warned. They would become immortal, autonomous beings. The woman was totally taken in by this speech and ate first before encouraging the male, who also ate. Lucifer gained victory by having his voice heard and obeyed, securing his rule within the hearts and minds of humans here on Earth.

Lucifer sought to establish himself above the Most High. Self-exaltation is the kingdom that he presides over in direct contradiction to the law of God, which is based on self-denial. Separated from God, Lucifer was already under the penalty of death before he occasioned the fall of humans. Jesus spoke of this during His ministry on earth, informing His disciples that hellfire was originally prepared for Lucifer and the angels who rebelled with him, not for humans (Matthew 25:41).

Lucifer is commonly known as the Devil, or Satan, which means opposer, adversary and slanderer. By occasioning the fall of humans, Lucifer has been given extra time to demonstrate what his rule would look like if he were the Most High. Undoubtedly, there would be no Earth left if God in his mercy and love for humanity did not make a way of escape by putting enmity between Lucifer and humans or the serpent and the woman. The enmity is the promised deliverer who would redeem mankind from their fallen state and restore humans to relationship and connection with God. The Word was made flesh and paid the penalty for man's disobedience, restoring our ability to choose. You see, as humans, we are still very ignorant regarding the true character and nature of God. Lucifer, however, is fully aware as he stood in direct proximity to

God. There is nothing further God can show Lucifer of Himself that would bring about repentance. But there is plenty God can show us humans of His love, the ultimate being His own sacrifice on the cross.

Closing Thoughts

I hope from this brief chapter you are beginning to get a glimpse of what is going on behind the veiled spiritual realm. Not only are humans having to contend with the consequences of disconnection from God, we also have spiritual enemies who are intent on keeping us under their influence. Through myriad schemes and plans these enemies continue to promote human self-sufficiency, keeping us from reconnecting to God and having our emotional need for His love met. Instead, the unmet emotional needs are manipulated to advance their kingdom of self-exaltation and self-worship. Sadly, we see this reflected in every facet of life. Jung, Freud, and others have successfully pulled the veil further by removing the spiritual understanding of the struggles we face every day. I would like to end this chapter with a reminder from the New Testament book, Ephesians 6:12: ***"For our struggle is not against flesh and blood, but against the rulers, against the authorities, against the powers of this dark world, and against the spiritual forces of evil in heavenly realms."***

Heart of the Gospel

PART 4:

The Gospel as the Cure.

Chapter 1:

Our Need for a Saviour God

The previous section attempted to provide a reason, from a biblical viewpoint, why humans experience painful emotional and psychological issues. We have inherited a sinful nature from our original human parents that has multiplied with every succeeding generation, from being born separated and alienated from God. The disconnection is now so wide that for the majority of us, we neither know, believe, or recognise that He exists. For those of us who do believe there is a God, we can be confused regarding his character and intentions towards us. Worship easily becomes a routine or ritual based on external instructions and not an intimate relationship. Some are motivated by the fear of being eternally punished forever in a fiery hell (a doctrine that is not supported by the Bible) or the hope of securing favour and prosperity.

The Issue of Justice and Mercy

Few people believe in and relate to God based on who He is – a God of mercy and justice, of love and holiness. A God who is ever compassionate yet will not allow the guilty to go without punishment. It is almost inconceivable to the human mind that justice and mercy can exist in the same person and be exercised at the same time. How can a judge execute justice by passing a sentence for a crime and yet allow the offender to walk away completely free in mercy?

And yet this is exactly what God does for each of us who respond to His call to come back to Him through the gospel message. In love, God exercises for us complete justice and complete mercy. How is this possible? Through the provision provided in His Son, the moment Adam chose to

Heart of the Gospel

disobey and forfeit the conditions for life. From that very moment, the Messiah has stepped in as our substitute to preserve human life, whether we believe in Him or not. This temporal life we enjoy is at the mercy and compassion of God, who has made death a temporary sentence for a time. Truthfully, when the first humans (Adam) sinned, in justice, they should have died permanently and all of us as their progeny should never have existed. But if it ended there, where would the demonstration of mercy be seen?

Moreover, human beings are so valuable to God that they cannot be cast off without hope of being redeemed. It is only into humans that God breathed part of His own Spirit and formed by His own hands. Every other part of creation was spoken into existence by the Word. With us, God went the extra nine yards... We are so valuable and precious to Him, even in our most hideous and fallen state. God created human beings with a spiritual nature that could be in an intimate relationship with Him. That plan has not changed.

In taking on human nature, God Himself entered physically into the human experience for the purpose of redemption, as He had covenanted (promised) to do. The death of Jesus Christ on the cross accomplishes two things. The first, securing eternal life and reconciliation for all who believe by faith and submit themselves to Him. The second, securing eternal death, the penalty chosen by all (both human and non-human) who choose to disbelieve and live in rebellion against God. The choice, as always, remains the same as in the beginning. Obey and live, disobey and die.

There has never been or ever will be a middle ground, something in our deceived and rebellious mind we are trying to accomplish on Planet Earth. Attempting to make our own way, our own kingdom using the natural resources of the earth that we did not make, to build our illusions of self-rule. The natural resources of the earth are manipulated by the few to oppress and subdue the majority. Even more so currently as we witness our rulers of nations attempting to form a one-world government.

Faith Is the Key

If we cannot accept by faith that God came in the same sinful flesh (nature) that we are born into and on our behalf paid the full penalty for sin by dying in our place, we have no hope of ever overcoming the inherited weaknesses and faults in that cause so much trouble. Our emotional and psychological needs can never be met to the degree they require without reconciliation with God. The human heart continues to "bleed" out. We are becoming more depraved, morally bankrupt and enslaved by our own lusts. We are becoming more lost as a generation. Today, anything and everything goes, leading to more confusion and delusions. Fear and anxiety are increasing as the lines between what is right and wrong are increasingly blurred. All of this is keeping us humans further in the dark about who God truly is and who we are in Him.

Chapter 2:

Why Evil and Suffering Exist

The purpose of this book is to present an alternative view of why mental health disorders are a common experience of human life and how they can be overcome from a biblical perspective. Modern medicine is rooted in the theory of evolution, which attempts to scientifically explain how this world and humans came to being and denies the existence of a Creator God who is self-existing and the source of all life.

The theory of evolution promotes atheism, the denial of a Supreme Being who is sovereign and has ordained all things for His glory. Evolution is the anchor on which humanism is founded – the belief humans have within them that they have the ability and capacity to solve their own problems, to carve out their own destiny, to be their own god, and have no need for a Saviour. Especially a Divine Saviour who seeks to offer us the way back into a relationship with God, whose government is founded on the principles of love, justice, and mercy.

The last statement is often laughed to scorn by many and used as the best argument against the existence of God. If the Supreme God who created this world is a Being of love, justice, and mercy, then why do evil and suffering exist? Why does He not prevent or stop the atrocities that are going on every day on Planet Earth? If such a being exists, how could they let things be this way? Many conclude that it is not possible for a God who declares Himself to be love to be true. So, they seek alternative answers.

Sadly, many professed believers and Christians fail to give an answer to this question or attempt to deflect it by stating God did not create evil. Such an answer reduces the sovereignty and all-knowing power of God to an afterthought in dealing with the issues of evil and suffering. They unintentionally present the idea that God is somehow on the back foot in dealing with this issue, or that He does not care about us. Deists have long advocated the idea that a Supreme Being indeed created the world and humans, but He has left His creation to be governed by humans and does not interfere with earthly affairs.

What Evil Really Is.

All of these ideas and others attempt to skirt around the reality. God *is* responsible for the existence of evil but did not ordain or choose for evil to be activated and be a part of our world by becoming attached to our human nature. Each one of us is a mixture of both good and evil. This is our natural fallen nature, inherited from the disobedience of Adam, the human parents of our race, from whom we are all descended. Evil is defined as the opposite or absence of good. The further away from good a thing or person is, the more evil they are described to be. Evil is a moral quality or attribute. In order for us to judge anything as being evil, we have to be aware of what the opposing quality or attribute is. In other words, what is good?

Our ability to discern between what is good and what is evil is in itself evidence that we are created beings with a moral conscience. In each of us, there is an awareness of God. A faint reflection of His law encoded within us. To discern evil, we must have some knowledge or idea of what good is. But in our fallen (self-centred) nature we attribute good to ourselves as something that we have evolved or developed because it is so intrinsic to us to be able to discern good from evil. But just as darkness really is the absence of light, and cold is the absence of heat, so evil is the absence of good, the absence of God.

The Gift of Free Will

How is it possible for God to be responsible for the existence of evil and not be responsible for its manifestation in all its forms? The answer is a simple yet very profound one. The answer lies in the principle of free will or choice. Not in the way this is understood and valued today, as the right to choose how one should be or live. Free will, or the ability to choose, is actually a lot more restrictive in its design, with greater consequences than having the right to freely express who or what we think we are.

Our free will or ability to choose operates within the narrow sphere of life and/or death. God created humans with the ability to choose to accept the conditions of life which is obedience through willing submission or not. The obedience and submission required are not arbitrary demands from a dictator. They are simply the means by which Man can remain connected to God who is the source of life.

As an example, think about the relationship between the plug and socket in our modern appliances. The socket is where the power of electricity is contained. The plug needs to be connected to the socket in order for the appliance to work, to be live. But another factor is essential. The socket needs to be switched on. The plug can remain connected to the socket, but if the socket is not switched on, no power can flow to the appliance and make it work (live).

Of course, this is a very simplified illustration, but I am sure you get the point. God is the source of life that we need to be plugged into in order to be spiritually alive, but the switch or our choice is what enables that life to continue. The more intelligent and advanced the created being, the more able they are to relate to God, to communicate and understand who He is.

Heart of the Gospel

Evil Is the Result of Choice

God is love and commands in love. Love cannot be compelled or forced, otherwise it loses the unique quality of freedom that it possesses. To make humans without the ability to freely choose to agree with the conditions of life is to make mere robots, incapable of individual thought and expression. In giving the creature (us humans) the capacity to understand and agree to submit to the conditions for life, the alternative is also created but latent.

At every step in creating the world as recorded in Genesis: 1, God pronounced each new addition as being good. All the physical, emotional, and psychological needs of man were supplied freely. Adam had complete dominion over the earth, but this was in response to their free will agreement to obey the one restriction placed on them.

The root word from which evil in the Hebrew language is derived actually means to spoil by breaking into pieces, to make worthless. Contrastingly, good means to exist, to be. God willed for this earth to exist, to be. But the principle of love warranted that the choice to agree with that existence is given to the creature with the devastating risk of the consequences should they choose not to, and this is what we are dealing with in our world today.

It would be natural to conclude that God made some error of judgment in allowing humans to have the deciding factor. Or that God did not foresee what could happen if Man chose to disobey. The reality is that God in His sovereignty already knew what would happen and chose in His wisdom not to prevent it for the eternal stability and well-being of all His creation, not just Earth.

Our Redemption Planned in Creation

From the very onset of creating our world, and with the foreknowledge of what would occur, God implanted within us and our world the principles of regeneration and redemption. God knew that Adam would make the choice to activate the "latent" evil through disobedience and bring death into the world. God foreknew that for a time, humans and this earth would be disconnected from Him, so the law or principle of reproduction was built into every living thing.

For a period of time, known only to Himself, God has allowed evil to exist. People often cry out and shake their fists to God because of the suffering and pain they feel. Others, as mentioned before, cannot believe that a loving God can allow such evil and not do anything, so they deny His existence. Some even dare to be bolder and deride the nature of God and place human wisdom and authority above the divine.

And all the aforementioned and more is done because we refuse to look at the truth. Yes, God does allow much suffering and evil in our world to exist, but He has not abandoned us. For those who choose to believe, they will see God working to redeem and restore. They will see the ultimate price God Himself paid in the suffering, death, and resurrection of Jesus. No other person or religious character is so mocked, derided and disrespected by all. Have you ever wondered why?

But who are we really to make such boastful and challenging assertions against the existence of God? Every natural resource on this planet is for our use, yet we do not make or do anything to sustain it. Despite the clearest evidence that speaks of Divine Intelligence, we dare to assert our poor substitute of evolution to explain our origins. The creature dares to mock the Creator because no lightning bolt zaps them. They use this as further evidence that God does not exist without understanding that it **IS** because God exists, they have the free will to do this.

The Choice Remains Ours

The principle of free will or choice is our gift from a loving Creator, who ensures the sun shines on the just and unjust alike. But there will come a time, a day when this demonstration of justice, mercy and grace will end. A time is coming when God will close this demonstration of rebellion and deal finally with the issues of evil, death, and disobedience. The Bible warns us this will be a fearful and terrible time for those who continue to deny His right to be Sovereign.

In contrast, God promises to all who choose to accept the conditions of life, a new heaven and earth where He will dwell with us. For those who believe in faith, death is but a temporary state to pass through. The principle of free will or choice to obey or disobey will remain, but no one who has been redeemed will choose to disobey having understood and experienced the knowledge of evil. In the certainty of God's will and presence, even evil itself is transformed into a useful tool to develop the image and likeness of God in us. The greater the darkness, the brighter the light shines for those who have spiritual eyes to see.

Chapter 3:

Living Temples and Sacrifices

Whenever we look at human civilisation, past and modern, no matter the culture or nation, we will find a common architectural theme: temples. These beautiful structures, in various shapes and forms, once stood in prominent places during ancient civilisations, as the centres of religious and social, legal, and economic power. Ask any archaeologist or anthropologist and they will delight in informing you of how the temples played a crucial role in the development and sustaining of prominent tribal groups such as the Incas and Aztecs, the Romans, and the Greeks, the Chinese and Egyptian dynasties. Or the Celtic and Nordic, Aboriginal and Native American sites. Medieval Europe replaced the temples with churches and cathedrals. Even in our modern times, the "temple" structure still holds together our legal and economic systems. We tend not to see it now, as the spiritual dimension has been hidden from our view by the guise of science and evolution. Modern man no longer needs to worship the gods, we can now explain everything with science. (We still do, we just do not realise we still do).

Modern Worshippers

Today, the temple has been replaced by football and sports arenas, cinemas, and theatres, shopping malls and markets, video games and computers. The biggest temple we all "bow down" before is none other than the grand TV. Through this medium (the majority of us have no clue how it works), we are given so many choices of programmes to be entertained with. We sit down to enjoy our favourite soap opera, drama, or movie without a thought about where this behaviour originated from. In ancient times, the temple services, rituals, and ceremonies often involved acting out the personalities or behaviours of the gods worshipped. Their personalities and behaviours were similar to our own human traits in character. In fact, there is a god for every aspect of human life. The gods themselves had their own drama-filled lives that were replayed before the worshippers and incorporated into their own lives. Today, we label these as myths and legends, but it is funny how these myths and legends keep popping up in our own scripts, Star Wars and Marvel to name a couple. Or watch some of the cartoons put out for our children with their strange characters from different places and time zones.

The point (that I have momentarily digressed from) is all ancient civilisations had some kind of temple service and sacrificial system, suggesting that at one point in time, humans held a common understanding of the Gospel, the plan for human salvation. This may seem like a bold assertion to make, but any honest study of ancient civilisations will reveal similarities and collective knowledge. They all worshipped the same gods, just gave them different names according to their language, and performed similar rituals for them. They all included a type of sacrificial system. The Aztecs, for example, would sacrifice their enemies by cutting out the heart and, while it was still beating, offer it up to the sun god they called Huitzilopochtli. Over in the area we now call the Middle East, the ancient Canaanite people were known to partake in child sacrifices to honour and appease their many gods, which included the well-known Baal, or Molech.

We may look back over our ancestral past and shudder at the brutality and ignorance of our forefathers, and with disdain conclude such barbaric acts were simply down to their primitive beliefs in God or the gods. Today, we have science that can explain what our ancestors believed were divine acts of supernatural beings. We now know how lightning strikes, and can predict weather patterns, and manipulate how things grow to ensure constant harvests.

Most religions have stopped or significantly reduced the use of animal sacrifices today. Historians conclude that sacrifices stopped because of the Age of Enlightenment during the seventeenth and eighteenth centuries, when people began to question and renounce the existence of God and instead promoted human reason and invention. The theory of evolution arose and expanded during this period and became the accepted version of how life began. But by the time evolution had spread, most of the sacrificial systems had already ceased by the spread of Christianity throughout the world.

The Conundrum of Justice vs Mercy

The sacrificial systems of ancient civilisations had a single starting point. As soon as Man chose to disobey and fall under the penalty of death, God offered Himself in His Son as the substitute. The justice of the law required death as the penalty. You see, life itself is under or controlled by laws. Every aspect of our human nature, spiritual, psycho-emotional, social, and physical, is governed by law. When we break these laws, there are consequences. Some after-effects are immediate, others take time to manifest.

The justice of the law of life could not be set aside in favour of mercy. A government with no order or enforcement would rapidly descend into chaos. If justice prevailed as it should, then where would mercy have its demonstration? How could God declare Himself to be merciful and gracious, if the penalty of death were immediately granted? This does seem to be a checkmate dilemma. It appears impossible for justice and mercy to be exercised at the same time, by the same person. And yet this is exactly what God has done every day and every time since the beginning. By giving Himself in place of man to pay the death penalty for transgression of His laws, God can also by the same virtue extend mercy and grace (second chance) to humanity. This temporary life that we so freely enjoy has been possible because of the Divine Sacrifice. The blood of the animal killed was a symbolic reminder.

Our first parents left the Garden of Eden with the promise of the redeemer. A gruesome object lesson was given to remind them that their lives were spared only because God promised to pay the price by taking on human nature and dying in their place. The sacrificial system was established to teach mankind the severity of transgressing the laws of life and the mercy of God in placing Himself as the ultimate sacrifice in our place. The promise of a divine redeemer, taking on humanity for this purpose, was given as recorded in Genesis 3:15, "I will put enmity between you and the woman and between your offspring and her offspring; he shall bruise your head, and you shall bruise his heel."

This statement was, in fact, made to the serpent, who had occasioned the fall of humans. By listening to the serpent's reasoning and distortion of the command God gave them to obey, Adam unwittingly chose the serpent as the one who should be obeyed. As discussed previously in Part 2: U*nderstanding our Spiritual Nature,* the human mind or spirit was not designed to be independent, but rather operate in connection with God to reflect His image and likeness. The capabilities God placed within the human spirit to complete His purpose have been hijacked by the serpent and continue to be, as long as humans believe they are fully independent and self-governing creatures. By taking on humanity, God has ensured each of us still has the ability to choose. This is why humans still have a moral conscience, and why we are a mixture of good and evil. If God departed from humanity completely, we would become a moral cesspit of decay and destruction before eventually dying without hope, just like a branch that physically decays and turns to dust. The human race would have ended soon after it began. You and I would not exist!

Righteousness: Man-made or God-given

Ever since the fall, humanity has been divided into two – those who believe by faith in the promises of God and seek to be restored back into relationship with Him by accepting the conditions of life, and those who do not. It has been debated who actually are the seed or offspring of the serpent. If you type this question into any search engine online, you will get loads of ideas or theories. The Bible makes it plain who the serpent's seed is, and it is an uncomplicated answer – anyone who rejects God, His will and authority, and substitutes His position with human ideologies and reasoning. Religious systems and practices are also divided into two: those who trust solely in the promises of God and choose to return in submission, giving up self-rule, and those who promote that eternal life can be earned by self-effort and self-belief. The latter, sadly, includes most of Christianity, which offers an "if you do X and don't do Y, you will be saved" deal.

By rejecting what God has revealed in His will, how righteousness (right standing with God and Man) can be obtained and going about this in our own way, or rejecting the notion that there is a God, to begin with, many are unknowingly obeying the voice of the serpent and by doing so, are considered his children. They remain naturally disconnected from God and more removed from His presence within, which only leads to increased narcissism, rebellion, fear, rejection, guilt, and shame exerting themselves on the human psyche. The less knowledge of God we have around us, the more evil dominates our nature, bringing with it psychological and physical ruin for many of us who cannot change the systems imposed on us.

Modern Temples and Priests

Psychiatry and psychology attempt to provide solutions and support in managing our mental distresses and dis-eases, but

Heart of the Gospel

because they are built on the premise of human self-sufficiency and deny the existence of God, they cannot treat the root causes. Instead, they often end up doing more harm by creating and furthering the belief that Man can solve his own problems and be his own god. A similar scenario to the temple systems of old times has been continued, but without the blood of animal sacrifices. In times past, when a moral issue was causing distress, or there were worries about prosperity, safety, or relationships etc., a person would come to the temple and request the service of the priests. They would come bringing a sacrifice which would be offered up to the gods. The worshipper would then be given instructions on what to do to ensure the outcome would be in their favour.

Today, in a comparable way, we turn to mental health professionals for support in managing our emotional and psychological distress. We rely on their counsel and follow their instructions. We take prescribed medications with no idea how they work, or of the potential side effects. In our science-based world, we have substituted the priest for the mental health professionals and doctors. We no longer bring a sacrifice, but a huge portion of our taxes or income is used to pay for their services. The pharmaceutical industry has made billions by making us dependent on their medications. Self-help gurus have also made a fortune by promoting their programmes, promising to make us better but ending up making them rich and their followers out of pocket with no lasting change to well-being. Sometimes we are left in a worse state.

The sacrificial and temple system was initially designed as an educational object lesson teaching mankind the root causes of our defective spiritual nature, and how in mercy God intends to restore all who will choose to submit themselves to His loving authority. As mentioned before, humanity has been divided into two categories – those that believe in faith, and those that do not. The Bible has kept a genealogy record of those who were given the responsibility of preserving the gospel in its sacrificial form until the Messiah, who was to fulfil all things, arrived. Today, we know them as the Jewish people. But remember this has always been an issue of *faith,* not genealogy, which explains why the majority of Jewish descendants do not accept Jesus as their prophesied Messiah. There are a minority who do, calling themselves Messianic Jews.

Why do I mention all this? In the following chapters of this section, I will attempt to outline what has been removed from the modern understanding of the Gospel. The Old Testament sanctuary or temple services formally started under Moses's leadership as a tent in the wilderness, developing into one of the wonders of the ancient world, the temple at Jerusalem. More importantly, I hope to briefly share how God works within us to restore us back into relationship and connection with Him. Human beings ARE the temple that God designed for Himself to dwell within.

Chapter 4

The Human Body is a Temple

Right from the beginning, humans were designed for the purpose of being directly connected to God; to be intimately connected to the Supreme Being, to be one with God and with each other as God dwells within each of us. Connection to God connects our spiritual nature to the source of life. This is the true way that our emotions (energy in motion) become regulated and flow through our physical bodies, encouraging health and well-being. It is the only way our inherent narcissism and rebellion can be truly subdued. Reconnection to God breaks the power of negative emotions, guilt, fear, shame, and rejection, lessening their destructive influence.

The Bible informs us that we are the temple of God (1 Corinthians 3:16). We were made as a dwelling place for the Holy Spirit of God, but through sin, the connection has been lost. The idea that the human body is designed as a temple is illustrated throughout the Bible. An example of this can be found in the construction and usage of the temple outlined in the Old Testament. The Jewish sacrificial system is the Gospel in symbols, foretelling the means God has provided for human salvation. In fact, it is hard to fully understand the Gospel as revealed in the New Testament without understanding why *this* system was established and the functions it provided.

A Brief Introduction and Overview

After delivering the nation of Israel from Egyptian bondage, God established His covenant with the nation and directed them to build a sanctuary, initially as a large tent, so that He could dwell among them (Exodus 25: 8). This sanctuary or temple building was an object lesson for us to understand how God intends to live within us. I will attempt to illustrate it below.

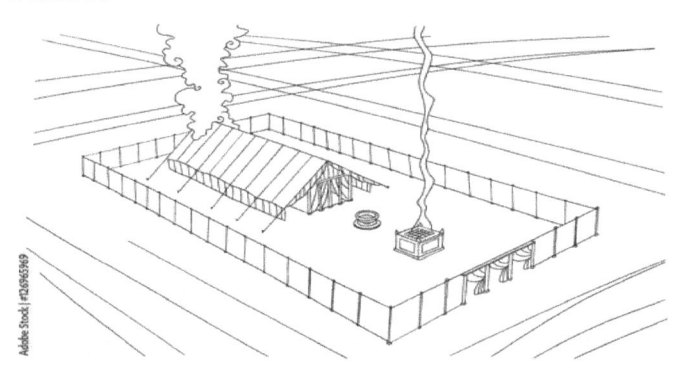

The Courtyard

The temple structure comprised two main sections, the Sanctuary building and the Courtyard, which was the immediate area around the Sanctuary building. The Courtyard was initially marked by a curtain boundary that was hung on pillars attached by tendons. Once the Jewish nation settled in the promised land after wandering in the wilderness, a permanent wall of bricks was created to mark the boundary wall of the Courtyard. Within the Courtyard was found the Altar of Sacrifice, where blood and animal offerings were made, and the Laver, which held water for cleansing.

The Courtyard has some similarities to our physical body. Our skin provides a definite boundary to contain what is within from what is outside. We have a skeletal system of bones upon which our skin is fastened via muscles. The Altar of Sacrifice and Laver could relate to the most physical of our senses, taste and touch. And just as the Courtyard could be observed and known by everyone, so, likewise, are we through our behaviours and words, manifested through our physical nature.

The Sanctuary

The Sanctuary, or Tabernacle as it was most commonly called, consisted of a single building that was partitioned by an elaborately woven curtain. This division created The Most Holy Place where the Ark of the Covenant and Mercy Seat (symbolising God's throne) were situated. Inside the Ark was the Ten Commandments, written by God on two stone tablets. Between the two Cherubim situated on either side of the Mercy Seat sat the Shekinah, or presence of God, in a cloud of light. On the other side of the partition was the Holy Place, containing the Altar of Incense, the Golden Candlestick, and the Table of Shewbread.

The Sanctuary building could symbolise our mind, or the spiritual nature that is within our physical body. The inner senses of sight, hearing and smell are represented here. Only the designated priest could enter the Holy Place on a daily basis. In a similar way, only you can really know what is going on in this part of your mind. It could be said that you (or me) are the designated priest. Psychology prefers the terms "ego" or "the self."

The Most Holy Place was even more restricted, with only the designated high or chief priest entering once a year. As mentioned before, the Most Holy Place is where the Shekinah or Divine Presence was seated. Underneath the Mercy Seat, or throne, where the Divine Presence emanated was the Ark of the Covenant, which contained the Moral Law or Ten Commandments, symbolising the government or rulership of God. No king or kingdom can exist without there being laws to promote order. The character of God is revealed and bound up within the existence of His Law. The Most Holy Place relates to the part of us that psychiatry calls the unconscious. Freud described the unconscious as the iceberg below the surface of conscious awareness, and the real motivator of our conscious actions.

Heart of the Gospel

The Problem with Us

The Ten Commandments that we are familiar with today are simply the amplification of that single instruction given in Eden, but now expressed in a manner that can be understood in our present fallen state, written on stone. Stone is considered to be a non-living substance unable to respond to living impulses. This makes stone a good example of how we in our natural state cannot respond appropriately to the spiritual promptings of the law within us. We are locked into the material/physical world (the real matrix), and more readily follow the external. We are born separated from God, as symbolised by the dividing curtain.

The human mind was designed to be the seat or throne where God resided, connecting us to Him, so that His image and likeness could be reflected. But we were not created as robotic beings. We were given the free will to choose, to accept the conditions of life, submission, and obedience by faith. And this is the main problem. In our fallen state, we cannot obey a spiritual command or law. Instead of God being seated on the throne within the Most Holy Place, the self is. And this is the root of the problem. We were not designed to be completely self-governing.

God's Solution

Reconnection to God involves us undergoing a spiritual new birth. Our spirit needs to be made alive again, to be renewed. This is the message of the Gospel, the good news of the Heavenly Kingdom. A way has been made that all who receive the Lord Jesus by faith can be born anew and be reconciled to God. During the time of the Sanctuary building in the Old Testament, daily sacrifices of animals were offered to represent the ultimate sacrifice God Himself would make to ensure reconciliation by satisfying the demands of justice screaming from the broken law. The Shekinah, or Divine Presence, through the Holy Spirit, can once again take precedence in the Most Holy Place, which relates to the deeper sensory processes of intuition, conscience, discernment, etc., influencing the motivations of our thoughts, imagination, emotions, and behaviours.

It was in the Most Holy Place that the presence of God resided, signifying where God desires to be within us; to give us true light and understanding; to regulate our senses and emotions by removing the darkness of separation caused by our inherited transgression of the Moral Law within us. To restore His Image by removing from us our sense of guilt, rejection, shame, and fear, and subduing our innate narcissism and rebelliousness. The gospel plan makes plain to us how this is accomplished through two steps that combine and continually work together. In Theology, they are called Justification and Sanctification. Does this sound religious and technical? It is not really. Please stick with me, you have made it so far.

Chapter 5:

Justification: Wiping the Slate Clean

Have you ever wished that you could start your life over again? To be able to undo mistakes made and make the right choice? Or avoid being hurt or taken advantage of? I am sure most of us have at some point wanted to go back and change something or cancel a decision. It is during these moments that the reality of life being a one-way street hits us. There is no going back into that past event that is affecting our present and shaping our future. We cannot take back the words spoken or actions done that have left us either in a state of remorse for our actions or trauma from someone else's. And being the fallen human beings we are, it is no wonder that we find ourselves a mixture of both. There are a few of us who refuse to acknowledge how their actions hurt others and do not appear to care if they do. But most of us, thankfully, still have sensitivity to the inner voice of conscience that lets us know we have done wrong to others and to ourselves. The problem is this inner voice of conscience in our natural fallen state is distorted and can become a source of much mental suffering.

Conscience vs Inner Critic.

A significant factor that separates human beings from the rest of the animal kingdom is that we have a moral conscience that governs our actions. Animals are led by bodily impulses and seasonal or environmental changes. An animal will find food when hungry or need to reproduce when in season, and defend its territory at all costs. A human can choose when to engage in all these actions and suppress the desire until the time is right. We humans operate under a higher principle than animals. We operate under morals or to soothe the scientists' principles and ethics. I am sure you are by now weary of me repeating that humans were created to reflect the image and likeness of God, but this really is the key issue. We are born out of sync with the divine law that is still encoded within us.

This law is always seeking for its aims to be met, the reflection of God in man. As fallen human beings, we are unable to meet the standard. A consequence of falling short is the critical inner voice of conscience inducing guilt for failing. Psychologists prefer the term "inner critic" and attempt to identify this voice as something separate from the voice of conscience, but the inner critic and the voice of conscience do the same thing. They both run the inner dialogue we all experience as the voice in our heads directing our behaviours. Conscience reminds us of what we should do or how we should be. The critic lets us know where we fall short and condemns us. Without the voice of conscience, there is no inner critic. Without Moral Law, there is no conscience.

Social order regulates how we behave as relational beings. All relationships are forms of social interactions that require the ability to connect and, in some types, form deep attachments. Whether we realise it or not, all social interactions are directed by Moral Law. Without Moral Law, there is no way humans could dwell together communally in a peaceful way. Societal norms and expectations are the modern way Moral Law is expressed externally. Self-esteem or self-worth is how Moral Law is expressed to the self, how we are living up to whatever the moral standards are, or societal norms and expectations.

Born with a Faulty Conscience

Conscience is what gives us the ability to discriminate between what is right and what is wrong and direct our behaviours accordingly. As humans, we are born with a conscience hard-wired into us, but it needs information to guide its operation. From the moment we are born, we are receiving instructions on how to conduct ourselves to be accepted, at first on a non-verbal or intuitive basis, which becomes more cognitive and rational as our brains develop and mature. However, this inbuilt conscience was originally "programmed" with the correct information to guide its operation. God designed and coded our conscience to align with His law or instructions on how to be like Him. As discussed in the previous chapter, the faint outline of this law is inscribed within each of us, but our fallen nature cannot respond as it ought to.

In fact, our fallen nature does the exact opposite of what is required. And every time we fail, we face the guilt-inducing voice of the inner critic, the shame of failure. We face the torments of fear and rejection. Being able to secure good enough attachments with our care givers does provide a muffler for the inner sense of condemnation, but it does not remove this completely. This is why despite having a good upbringing and success in life, we still inwardly struggle with not being good enough or doing right. In loving and supportive relationships, we learn to have a more positive view of ourselves. We are better able to push back against the inner critic and rationalize negative emotions. For those of us who have unfortunately been raised in an environment that could not provide a secure attachment pattern or protection from harm, there is less defence from the negative emotional states of fear, shame, rebellion, narcissism, rejection, and guilt. The inner critic seems constant in voicing its negative tirade. The milieu appears to confirm rather than deny the reality of how fallen we are, without providing any means of comfort or hope.

Self-Justification

The inner critic, or the voice inside our heads that tells us we are not right or have not done something right, drives us to try and make ourselves right, to do better. As children, we were dependent on the adults around us for survival. We needed at all costs to stay in connection with them, to form some kind of attachment. These biological drives are hardwired to us motivate us to conform, to make ourselves right. The need to justify or be right continues throughout our lifespan. At every stage of our lives, we are faced with societal and legal expectations, telling us how well we are measuring up, and how right we appear in the eyes of others. The challenge is the standards and expectations are always shifting or changing. What is right today is no longer right tomorrow. Think of our ever-changing world of fashion as an easy example. Yet despite how well we might conform our lives to the required standard, it never is enough to take away that inner sense of something missing, not being quite right. We oscillate between projecting our inner sense of unworthiness onto other people or imploding in episodes of harsh self-criticism.

Even those who appear to go against societal and legal expectations are doing the same thing in a negative way, by trying to bypass or reject the expectations that they know deep down they cannot meet. When we believe we cannot meet the expectations, we employ safety behaviours such as avoidance, aggression or isolation, as seen in anxiety and mood disorders. Some, from a young age have decided it is impossible and they withdraw into the safety of becoming mentally unwell. This may appear a harsh thing to state but after years of working within mental health services, I have noticed a common theme. There are people who have simply given up trying to meet the ever-changing expectations needed to stay attached and accepted. They have chosen to withdraw mentally as an act of self-preservation, escaping the pressures of failing both externally and internally.

Unmet emotional needs are understood to be the basis of addictions and impulsive behaviours. All forms of personality disorders have their roots in insecure attachment patterns from childhood. The more disruptive and traumatic our early years have been, the more likely we will go on to develop physical and mental health issues as adults. The further away as a society we move from having clear standards of what is right and wrong that are enforced, the more we descend individually into mental and emotional chaos, trying to make our own selves right and accepted even at the expense of another person's rights. We become more rebellious, narcissistic, fearful, ashamed, guilt-ridden, anxious, and rejected as we try harder to justify ourselves and make ourselves right. Social media has made it so easy for us to deceive ourselves and others; to build fantasy worlds where we can escape into our own perfection, taking us further away from the reality of who we really are.

Only God can Justify us

Behind the drive to justify ourselves is the fear of death. The final death is the end of life itself, but death sends out its forerunners in the form of separation or loss. From the moment we are born, we are engaged in the fight to exist, to stay relevant to others and live as long as possible. Typically, we do not think of our death, which enables us to go about our daily affairs and make future plans with confidence. That is until in some form, we come face to face with the fragility of life. Despite the many methods humans have devised to make themselves right, to stave off or make peace with the sentence of death, using religious or scientific means, death still remains the final outcome for every living thing.

The conditions for eternal life have not changed. God still requires obedience by faith in His Word and submission to His sovereignty as the One who has the right to rule. By offering Himself as the ultimate sacrifice, God demonstrates to us His everlasting love and mercy. "The Word was made flesh and dwelt among us" (John 1:14).

Heart of the Gospel

As incredible as this may sound, the very Word of God was placed in human form, not as an abstract idea, but as a living breathing entity that has the capacity to enter into our human experience. The Word was made flesh... meaning that the promised Messiah or deliverer is both human and divine. It was the divine Word of God that pronounced death as the penalty for disobedience to male Adam at the beginning. This death is eternal, but through God's mercy and self-sacrifice, death is, for now, a temporary state. The Bible speaks clearly of a day of judgement, of reckoning, where all the dead will be raised to life again. Some to the resurrection of life, others to the resurrection of damnation from which there is no return (John 5: 28-29).

But the subject of the final day of judgement is a huge topic in itself that cannot be dealt with here. Suffice it to say that deep within our subconscious, we know that there is something beyond death and it is this "knowing" which causes us to live in fear by attempting to manage or eliminate any form of uncertainty, any form of separation from our lives. Fear of death or separation underpins every anxiety disorder diagnosed.

Justified by the Death of Jesus

It is funny today how we can entertain Greek and other myths that depict "the gods" taking on human form or having relations with human females, producing hybrid offspring with extraordinary strengths and abilities. In our modern world, we call them superheroes. The Marvel franchise has made billions selling this idea to us in their movies and comics over the years. ***Yet we find it almost impossible to believe that God Himself came to earth in human form.*** The idea of God taking on a human form is not unique to Christianity. In Hinduism, the god Rama is understood to be the human embodiment of Vishnu, one of the supreme gods in the Hindu pantheon (which, incidentally, has comparisons with the Greek and Roman equivalents).

The major difference between the incarnations is that in Christianity, God became flesh for the purpose of redemption. By paying the death penalty for human disobedience, the slate is wiped clean. Mankind can be reconciled back into a relationship with Him. God came as human to demonstrate perfectly that His law is just and can be obeyed. The nature of His kingdom is love, which requires self-denial, putting the benefits and well-being of others first. God demonstrates this continually by sharing His life, sustaining all of His creation, and giving His life on the Cross. The Gospel is the message of God's redeeming love for every descendant of Adam who, by faith, chooses to believe. No matter who we are or what we have done, we can have a new start.

Without this love, the human heart is driven to seek fulfilment in the material world. But this world cannot supply this need for love completely. The human heart without God is driven by the uncontrolled innate drives we have inherited in our fallen nature. Only by accepting the provision that God in Himself has provided can we begin to find true inner peace, silencing the condemning voice of the inner critic and the subduing of our innate drives. This gift of grace is free, but not without some cost to us. We first have to admit that there is a Creator God that we are in rebellion with through our natural birth. We secondly have to accept the painful truth; we also have sinned against Him. Thirdly, we must choose or want to agree with the conditions of life, obedience, and submission. All three actions are summed as repentance towards God which justifies us. They also go hand in hand with the next step, sanctification.

Chapter 6:

Sanctification: The Divine Image Restored.

So, just to recap briefly, justification simply means that the slate has been wiped clean. Through the death of Christ, humanity has been released from the penalty of eternal death as chosen by our first parents, Adam. The way has been opened for us to be reconciled to our Creator and be in a relationship with Him again. The spiritual realm of the kingdom of Heaven, where God dwells, is now accessible to us. We have been redeemed and made right. Surely this is fantastic news. The early believers thought so and spent their lives spreading this great news, the Gospel, across the world. No other belief system has had a greater impact on changing societies and uplifting the human race as genuine belief in the Gospel. Whether we realise it or not, the Gospel has majorly transformed our world and still provides the framework for our modern society, especially in the West.

I emphasise genuine belief or faith in the Gospel on purpose to make a distinction between the straightforwardness of simple faith and the ritualized form that now identifies itself as Christianity. The essence of the Gospel has been lost under the ever-growing mound of ceremonies, money-grabbing endeavours, and the hypocritical self-righteousness of many who profess to be Christians. The Christian Church historically has been (and still is) guilty of committing in the name of religion, many inhumane acts of cruelty against those who do not believe or accept their self-imposed right to rule the conscience. The Christian Church today, in most of its forms, is so far removed from the simplicity and love of the Gospel message that once empowered it. It is not surprising that many people today choose to disbelieve, citing the lack of difference today between a Christian and non-Christian. If there is any difference, it is merely that one verbally states they believe but there is no alteration in attitudes and behaviours.

Diluting The Gospel

In preaching the Gospel message today, the emphasis seems to centre on love. Now please do not get me wrong, love IS the essence of the Gospel. It surely is because of love for humanity that God humbled Himself and entered into our world as a human being to die, instead of just wiping us out in justice. But this is only half of the story. The other half is bound up in the actual life God lived while a human being in the flesh. We may find it hard to grasp, accept or understand what is meant by God living as a human, entering into our experience, but if we do not, we miss entirely the other half of the Gospel message. Jesus came to not only die, but to cancel out the debt stacked against us. While on earth, Jesus lived a life that overcame our inherited narcissism, rebellion, fear, shame, rejection, and guilt. He faced all the hardships and sufferings we experience, living in a fallen world.

It would be a tremendous downgrade for God to come to this earth and live in the most expensive and luxurious palace Man could build. He created everything, including us! Yet we learn that Jesus bypassed the homes of the wealthy and came into this world homeless. He who is rich beyond all measure, entered into our world as one of the poorest. From the very beginning, He was rejected, abused, and maligned even by His own natural family members (Mary and Joseph did go on to have more children). His own countrymen refused to believe who He was and, in the end, turned Him over to the Romans to suffer the most excruciating execution known. The Lord suffered physical, mental, emotional, financial, and potential sexual abuse.

Unlike the common portrayal of Him dying on the cross with a loin cloth covering, the reality is that Jesus hung on the cross naked! Today we would identify anyone who has been forcibly stripped naked publicly as a victim of sexual assault. It is a known historical fact that the Romans made death by crucifixion as painful and humiliating as possible to ensure that their rulership over the then-known world was complied with. Malefactors were crucified naked and left to writhe in pain while being mocked and jeered by the public. It may be hard to imagine that the Creator God would allow the creatures He has made to treat Him so awfully without resistance. But He suffered all this and more, not just to die, but to put His life into fallen humanity so we can overcome the inherited rebellion, narcissism, guilt, shame, fear, and rejection we all have. It is not just the death of Jesus that saves us. We are saved also by accepting His life, and His ways instead of our own.

Sanctification: The Other Half.

Accepting or believing that God came in human form and died for us is one half of the Gospel. To know that all sins committed are wiped out and humanity has been made right with God is one thing. To benefit from this is another. Indeed, the famous words of John 3:16 state, "For God so loved the world that He gave His only begotten Son, that whosoever believes in Him should not perish, but have eternal life". The world truly for all ages has been reconciled to God, but we receive this on an individual basis. God deals with each of us on a one-to-one basis. Let me put it this way for an illustration of this point. A declaration is made on the news that every citizen in the town has deposited a million pounds into their bank account. The only way the money can be withdrawn is if each person goes to the bank and proves their identity. Most people think it is a hoax and refuse to go. Some do but do not take identification with them. They learn the money is there, but they cannot access it. A smaller group believe and take identification with them. They are able to withdraw from the account.

The money is there but you have to comply with the conditions to receive it. You have to bring your identification, or your identity, to the bank. In response, you are able to withdraw from your personal account. It cannot be accessed by anyone else. In a similar way, God has made salvation available to every single person, but we can only access this on an individual basis by complying with the conditions stipulated. Our identification in this instance is repentance as outlined at the end of the previous chapter. We have to admit that there is a Creator God that we are born separated or disconnected from through our natural birth. We must accept the painful truth that we also fail to meet the mark and sin against Him. We choose or desire to choose to agree with the conditions of life, obedience, and submission.

The next step is agreeing to give up our natural life in order to accept the new life (spirit) that God offers to give us. The life that He worked out for us in humanity before dying as our substitute. We ought to never forget that the God of mercy who died for us is also the God of justice. Death is still lurking around, seeking its due. Those who accept the provided solution are spared the eternal consequence of death. To those who do, death is a temporary state. Just as Jesus rose again from the grave to eternity, so will all who have accepted His life and consented for the Divine Image to be restored in them. But that new life, the restoring of the Divine Image has to be done in the here and now. This is the process of sanctification, the big clean-up of our lives for the rest of our natural lifespan. It can be a difficult process at times, but the immediate rewards are immense, and we have the promise of eternity too.

New Spirit, Old Brain.

The death of Jesus satisfies the outstanding claims of justice that sit on the head of every human being who is born into

Heart of the Gospel

the "matrix" only as they accept by faith the conditions of true repentance. By faith, God renews our spirit so that we can be in connection with Him again. We begin to have new desires and impulses bringing about changes in our behaviours. As we learn to spend time with God through meditating on scripture and speaking to Him in prayer, we come to know and understand who He is and who we truly are. Like any new experience or relationship, there is that initial phase of excitement and joy we want to share with others. They may even notice positive changes in our personalities. But at some point, this initial phase or bubble begins to wear off as the daily challenges of life impose upon our new experience or relationship.

Repentance and justification before God renew our mind (spirit), giving us peace within. This change takes place within the old brain that contains all the stored memories. The brain, as wonderful and essential as it is, remains part of the physical or natural nature and is still fallen. The brain has been naturally wired through genetics and lived experiences to operate in ways that are opposite to what God commands. Our brain (and body) still responds to the "sinful" environment because we still continue to live.

When, through repentance, we accept the death of Jesus on our behalf, we agree to give up our life in exchange for the life He secured for us while living as a human before dying. We accept His death in place of ours and consent for the old nature to die, so we can receive the new life from Him. But this new spiritual life does not come separate from Jesus. By faith, we become united or attached to Him.

Going back to the previous illustration of the million-pound bank deposit – in order to claim the deposited funds, you have to bring proof of your identity in order to begin withdrawing from the account. The conditions are that you give up or submit your identity in exchange for access to withdraw from the account. In accepting the offer God provides for salvation, you agree to give up your natural sinful self-life in exchange for His own. You agree for the Divine Image to be restored within through intimate relations and connection with Him. Jesus is the account, and the money (life) does not come separate from Him. Going back to the illustration, we remember there were some who came to the bank but did not bring proof of their identity. This group represent those who believe in the Gospel but do not comply with its conditions. They profess to be believers or Christians, but they do not give up their natural self-life. There is no true change. In fact, they are a lot worse than those who do not believe. They are hypocrites and turn many away from accessing the true healing desperately needed.

New Life Grows Within the Old

In accepting the death of Jesus on our behalf, we also accept His life within us. The Spirit of God enters into our spirit, bringing new life and purpose to us. This is referred to as new birth or being born again. There indeed should be changes in our desires and inclinations, but we also find ourselves being pulled by old habits and behaviours. These old habits and behaviours are coming from the "ghost" of the old you, still encoded within the neural pathways of the brain and somatic memories in the body. Sanctification is the lifelong process of overcoming our natural, dysregulated drives. No easy feat, as the world is built to provide for and sustain our appetite, thirst, reproduction, and self-preservation independent of God.

Self-preservation is our threat response, constantly triggered by being in a world where death resides. Humans have long understood the power that our natural drives have over us. By controlling natural resources and limiting free access, people have been able to enslave their fellow humans and control how societies should function. The rich and powerful few preserve themselves at the expense of the masses. Our dysregulated drives in our natural state produce

Heart of the Gospel

what the Bible terms the "fleshly lusts" according to 1 John 2:16. Lust is defined as *epithumeo,* from the Greek language, meaning to "set the heart upon, to long for." Now, having desires is not in or of itself a bad thing. In fact, if you recall the laws of the mind discussed earlier in Part 2: **Understanding our Spiritual Nature**, to hope or desire is a law of the mind. It is where the desire is coming from or what the desire or lust is wanting to obtain. *Epithumeo i*s taken from the root *Epi,* which means to superimpose relating to time, place, or order. To superimpose is to put something over something else.

The inherent drives of appetite, thirst, reproduction, and self-preservation are what direct the behaviours and decisions of men instead of the commands or law of God, which is cast aside and broken in order to satisfy these needs. Without a reconnection to God in our spiritual nature, we are led primarily by our physical drives. These same unregulated physical drives are the source of inner conflict when we become reconnected to God. Sanctification is the process of subduing or regaining control and dominion of our personal selves and our personal environment. Everything needs to come under submission to the will and reign of our Divine Creator, through sustained intimate relationship by choice, just as it was at the beginning. A choice we make moment by moment, every day.

Human Will Power is not Sufficient

Asceticism is Man's attempt to control our natural inclination to obey our physical lusts by means of firm self-discipline and denial, seek in our own strength to overcome and reverse the sinful effects of the fall. This is the primary intention behind all religions that promote a "rule-based" way of life such as Judaism, Islam, Buddhism, Hinduism, Catholicism, and other forms of Christianity. Following their rules and guidance may appear to give an outward show of holiness or rightness, but they are unable to change the sinful direction or superimposition of the physical over the spiritual. The world has been exposed to countless revelations of sexual misconduct and cruelty in such religious organizations. Therapy is the humanistic attempt to do the same using scientific understanding to change thinking patterns and behaviours. Therapy, while having some merit, also falls short of effecting lasting change because, like religion, therapy relies on human willpower alone. Such efforts are not able to satisfy the emotional needs for divine love that are hardwired in us – the Divine Love that is extended to all of us through the unlimited bounty of forgiveness.

Chapter 7:

The Power of Forgiveness

It would be really remiss to conclude this final section without discussing the most crucial part of the Gospel message, forgiveness. Forgiveness is the branch on which justification and sanctification hang. Without the forgiveness of God, we cannot be reconciled back into a relationship with Him. Without the ability to forgive others and our own selves, we are unable to experience true emotional and psychological health. The peace of mind we crave, the sense of certainty and assurance we seek will elude us. The topic or issue of forgiveness is quite delicate and often misconstrued. As long as we live in this fallen world, we will face situations where we either need to forgive an offence against us or be forgiven for offending another person.

These hurts or offences multiply often to the point where they affect our ability to function. We are led to seek psychological and emotional support for the offences against us that cause us to feel traumatic pain. Many of us refuse to let go of the hurt another has inflicted. Science has proven that unforgiveness can trigger physical and mental illnesses, leading to the development of various therapeutic techniques on how to forgive. Forgiveness, or the act of forgiving, in itself is a powerful mechanism for change and healing. Not because it has been scientifically proven, but because it is part of the higher moral law(s) that governs us as humans. And every act of genuine forgiveness comes from a higher source than us. The ability to forgive is the gift God has given to us as part of His solution to save and redeem us. Every genuine act or decision to forgive is evidence that God exists, whether we believe in Him or not. A bold assertion indeed to make, but those of us who have experienced the power of forgiveness recognise a quality that is more than human.

Forgiveness Originates with God

The first thing we need to realise about forgiveness is that we can only extend it to offences that are moral or involve moral qualities, by the very definition of the term "offend" which means to "transgress, violate, or cause a person to feel hurt or resentment." Every living person, no matter who or where they are born, functions under some form of moral law. It is impossible not to be moral as this is what makes us human. Our code of conduct may vary according to place of birth and other factors, but we all operate under the last six commandments that govern human-to-human interactions. There is no society, however primitive, that does not have some guidelines around stealing, murder, the right to own possessions, or family/social relationships. Violations of these rules bring penalties upon the offender.

Every human offence is simply the repetition of Adam's choice to go against the command God gave to them right at the beginning. The moment Adam chose to disobey was the moment that God chose to forgive. God chose to "*give*" His life "*for*", or in exchange for, Adam's (humanity). Forgiveness is not something that is without cost. Every offence against the Moral Law, which is the Law of Life, requires the death of the offender. The twin issues of justice and mercy are played out every time. We demand ***justice*** or payback when wronged against. We ask for ***mercy*** or compassion when we have done wrong. This is the whole crux of our legal system; why, we even attempt to provide a defence for the one who is without doubt guilty! This conflict between justice and mercy is resolved only in One and by One. It has been resolved by God Himself, in Himself. Every human act of genuine forgiveness is the outworking of divine forgiveness within the human, the source of its power to heal and restore. The emphasis is placed on genuine forgiveness because genuine forgiveness comes with a cost.

The Cost of Letting Go

Whenever another person hurts or offends us, a moral debt is generated. If the offence is seen as being minor with little damage or harm to us, we find it easier to cancel the debt and let the offence go. If the offence or hurt has significantly impacted our life, the harder we find it to let the offence go. We demand some form of justice or acknowledgement from the person. We require that person to pay us what we are owed. Certain offences or crimes against us warrant a custodial or prison sentence. All offences require open recognition of what was done. We need the person to own up and apologise. We need them to admit they have wronged us. The debt keeps pressing on us and we cannot cancel it without giving up our rights for justice. We want, we need that person to settle the score, to pay the price for us to let go, to forgive. Until they do, we will hold them to account.

The problem is the offender cannot fully repay us the debt owed. Some debts can never be repaid, such as taking the life of a loved one, undoing abusive acts or anything that leads to a permanent consequence for the victim. Even when the offender does admit their wrongs to us, the damage to our emotional and psychological health is so overwhelming, that we struggle to let the offence go. We still want what is morally due to us and cannot forgive. What we do not realise is that our cry for justice is a demand for the life of the offender. This is the real price we want that offending person to pay. Most people would resist this truth and deny that they want the offender to die. But if we dare to be honest, we will agree that they should not be allowed to continue living a good successful life. Their life should be filled with misfortune. They do not deserve to be happy. We may not want them to physically die, but we certainly do not want them to enjoy life either.

Forgiveness is the act of mercy or compassion towards the offending person who rightly does not deserve this. To truly forgive means cancelling the moral debt owed to us. It means giving up our rights for justice. If they have committed a criminal offence against us, they should be brought to face criminal charges. Forgiveness does not mean that just dues should not be paid. Criminal offences are not only against the individual but against the public too and should be addressed. Society would descend into chaos if there was no outer system of enforcement to punish those who break the moral law or act as a deterrent for those of us who would break it. What is being addressed here is the spiritual nature, the inner part of us. Even when the offender has been found guilty and given a long prison sentence or in some countries put to death, we can still struggle to forgive, to let go. The offender has not been able to give back the peace, the innocence, the life we had or should have had. They cannot take away the emotional and psychological pain out of the memory. We, the victims, have to choose to release them completely. But where is the moral justice in doing that? Who is going to pay me back for these losses? Another human being cannot. Only God can.

True Forgiveness is Divine not Human

True forgiveness requires the complete release of the offence and the offender of what is morally owed ***without*** the acknowledgement or attempts to repay by them. True forgiveness requires the victim to have a fair understanding of what this is going to cost them. They understand that by choosing to give up their rightful claims for justice they are prepared to suffer the loss of never being compensated. They also determine not to respond or retaliate in any way that shows that the debt is still outstanding. A decision is made to not bring the offence back up repeatedly. It is over, it is done. True forgiveness requires self-denial or sacrifice and self-discipline. Forgiveness is a cognitive or rational act of the will. It is not emotionally led but will in time soothe the emotions by allowing the hurt emotions space to be expressed. True forgiveness leads the person offended to bless and genuinely wish the best for the offending person.

Another thing that forgiveness enables us to do is understand or try to understand the perspective of the offender. As crazy as this may sound, it is actually true. In genuine forgiveness, there is some recognition of the life challenges faced by the offender. This is not an excuse and should not be taken as an excuse. True confession or repentance recognises that there is no excuse for the hurt or harm we have caused others. There may be external factors, but true repentance acknowledges it was a choice or decision made to do XYZ. No attempt to justify self here. True forgiveness recognises that we hurt others also. Maybe not in the same way or extent, but nevertheless we do, and for these offences, we also need to be forgiven. Whenever we truly seek to forgive another person, we begin to activate the release of divine love and power into our own lives and the lives of others. How many criminals who have made a life from hurting and manipulating other people, come to know the truth of who God is through the extension of genuine forgiveness to them by their victims?

The Debt We All Owe God

It is often during the times that we have been seriously wronged or done wrong that our thoughts turn towards God, mostly to express doubts about His existence or love for allowing this to happen to us. But the marvellous thing is that God does hear our cries and sees beyond the bitterness and anger to the emotional pain. If, during these times of vulnerability, we open ourselves up to God, we will find that both the victim and offender meet in the same place. We begin to realise that forgiveness does not extend only from human to human, but upward from humans to God. We begin to grasp the significance of the cross, not as a story or symbol, but as a living reality. The debt that we individually owe our Creator is far greater than any debt another human being can owe us.

The first four commandments of the Moral Law relate to our relationship with God. The painful truth is that we break the six commandments that relate to our human-to-human interactions because we have *all* broken the first four, simply by being born. How tragic a state we humans are in. We all naturally put ourselves in God's place or deny His existence. We worship and praise the idols of our own efforts and achievements, great or small, communal, or individual. We obey our own desires and wants, placing the human above the divine. We misrepresent or take in vain the name or character of God by reflecting a distorted image full of rebellion, narcissism, fear, shame, guilt, and rejection instead of love. We continue to destroy peace and harmony wherever we go. The natural world has no peace or rest and is constantly abused because of us. We each owe the Divine Creator a debt that we cannot pay.

And yet, despite all of this, if we turn back to God in true repentance, we will find that we have already been forgiven. The death of Jesus on the cross has paid for every outstanding debt humanity owes and satisfies the claims of justice. This allows mercy to be freely given to each of us. We cannot earn this gift. It is deposited in our individual account the moment we are born and remains there until we begin drawing from our account after meeting the requirements as discussed previously. We can only genuinely forgive because we have been forgiven. Forgiveness is the gift God has given us by His death, which enables us to continue living together in our fallen nature. God so loved the world He *gave* His Life *for* ours, right from the start.

A Final Note to End On

We often mistake forgiveness for reconciliation. If we have really forgiven the offender, we should treat them normally and have no hard feelings. Forgiveness is distorted to mean we minimize what has happened and continue being in connection with the offender(s). This is particularly accurate with family members, but this is not true forgiveness. True forgiveness acknowledges the wrong committed, the emotional hurt from the offence and addresses the issues. Forgiveness involves releasing the debt owed, but there is no expectation to stay in connection with the offender. In fact, it could be dangerous to do so and impossible to heal from. Morally, it is also unacceptable as we end up only enabling the offender to hurt us more if they do not recognise they are hurting us and repent or change their actions. If they do not admit and change their actions and we choose to stay, the relationship becomes dishonest, providing the perfect ground for bitterness and unforgiveness to grow. Instead, we should try and distance ourselves from them or place boundaries where we cannot.

God Himself has set the example of this. He has forgiven every one of us. We are born with a sinful nature we did not choose, but we cannot enter into a close relationship with Him unless we repent and choose to accept the divine exchange of His life for ours. Every relationship is subject to moral conditions or laws that must be respected and adhered to. The violation of the Moral Law encoded within us is the true reason we experience emotional and psychological issues. Unforgiveness plays a huge role in their maintenance, a primary cause why attempts to cure illnesses of this nature fail and will continue to fail. Life is spiritual. We ignore this fact at our peril.

Heart of the Gospel

Heart of the Gospel

Milton Keynes UK
Ingram Content Group UK Ltd.
UKHW021216010424
440357UK00005B/79

9 781835 631409